10 Years of Regulation 1/2003: Challenges and Reform

GCLC Annual Conference Series

College of Europe
Collège d'Europe

Brugge | Natolin

Global Competition Law Centre

6

10 Years of Regulation 1/2003: Challenges and Reform

GCLC Annual Conference Series

Edited by
Massimo Merola, Nicolas Petit and José Rivas

bruylant

Pour toute information sur nos fonds et nos nouveautés dans votre domaine de spécialisation, consultez nos sites web via www.larciergroup.com.

© Groupe Larcier s.a., 2015
Éditions Bruylant
Espace Jacqmotte
Rue Haute, 139 - Loft 6 - 1000 Bruxelles

Imprimé en Belgique

Dépôt légal
Bibliothèque nationale, Paris : octobre 2015
Bibliothèque royale de Belgique, Bruxelles : 2015/0023/211

ISSN 2294-5571
ISBN 978-2-8027-5294-3

TABLE OF CONTENTS

■

I

PROCEDURAL CONVERGENCE IN ANTITRUST ENFORCEMENT – A PERSPECTIVE FROM THE INSIDE

II
PROCEDURAL CONVERGENCE IN ANTITRUST ENFORCEMENT – IN NEED OF INCREASED COHERENCE AND EFFECTIVENESS?

III
MODERNISATION 2.0 – OUTSTANDING ISSUES

FOREWORD

■

Massimo Merola, Nicolas Petit and José Rivas

This book contains the proceedings of the 2014 Annual Conference of the Global Competition Law Centre (GCLC). The GCLC was created back in 2004 within the law department of the College of Europe (CoE). This is the sixth volume of the GCLC Annual Conference Series.

The 2014 GCLC annual conference was dedicated to Regulation No. 1/2003 and its first ten years of implementation. More specifically, the conference sought to explore the various issues that arise during the life-cycle of cases that fall within the scope of Articles 101 and 102 TFUE. Once more, the GCLC attempted to achieve its mission statement, which is not only to host brain-storming events between enforcers and high-level practitioners and academics, but also – and above all – to put forward ideas for the improvement of antitrust law and policy in the European Union.

The 2014 conference was built on the positive outcome of a series of decentralised Lunch-Talks organised by the GCLC in France, Italy and Poland throughout 2013 and 2014, which allowed the gathering of empirical data on the implementation of Regulation No. 1/2003 at national level.

Former Director-General of DG COMP Philip Lowe, one of the architects of Regulation No. 1/2003, graciously agreed to give the keynote speech to open the conference. This speech, which is reproduced in this volume, provides a retrospective insight on the modernisation of the competition rules introduced by Regulation No. 1/2003.

The conference was structured in two main parts. In the first part the speakers were asked to analyse the Commission's Communication and Staff Working Paper, particularly in relation to the timeless question of procedural convergence in antitrust enforcement (session one).

In this regard, Philip Marsden explained that there are limits on leniency convergence, due to a lack of harmonised sanctions. He also stressed that the detection rate in the UK is higher than ever and is expected to continue increasing following the appointment of a director of intelligence within the CMA. Professor Marsden also addressed the danger of pushing for too much agency independence and stressed that the main issue is accountability. In Philip Marsden's view, performance based review by the government is not, on its face, antagonistic to independence. He also urged for more transparency, particularly with respect to providing clear reasoning in non-infringement, no-grounds for action and commitment decisions. His session closed with a discussion of case allocation and proposed the creation of a multinational task force for cases that affect several national markets and where expertise is spread among different NCAs.

Once the general questions addressed by the Commission were set out, Laurence Idot and Denis Waelbroeck tackled the specific issue of the investigation of cases by antitrust agencies. Professor Idot focused on the power of NCAs to set priorities for the initiation of investigations and proceedings in relation to individual cases. More specifically, she analysed the rightfulness of the Commission's assertion that: "*there is a need for further convergence on the ability of the authorities to set priorities when choosing which cases to pursue*" and drew a comparison between two systems, the prioritisation-based system, favoured by the Commission (applied in Northern Europe), and the system based on the legality principle, which triggers a legal duty to consider all complaints (adopted in France and Italy). Mrs Idot concluded that convergence of procedural rules within the ECN is, of course, one objective, but not the main one.

Denis Waelbroeck instead assessed the degree of procedural convergence across Member States. He discussed issues such as legal professional privilege, disclosure of evidence by antitrust agencies, inspections and requests for information. The analysis revealed that there are worrying inconsistencies and, thus, advocates harmonising initiatives by the ECJ under the principle of effectiveness and within the ECN through mandatory legislative acts.

Effectiveness in antitrust enforcement was the focus of session two, during which it became clear that the need for convergence also applies when the Commission and NCAs issue decisions. As acknowledged by Mario Siragusa, Regulation No. 1/2003 has positively contributed to harmonising competition law within the EU. However, divergences remain from a procedural standpoint, which reduce legal certainty and often increase legal costs for undertakings, thus entailing a highly detrimental impact on businesses operating within the EU. Mario Siragusa therefore concluded that the major challenge facing Member States – both individually and in the forum of the European Competition Network – for the next ten years will be to achieve further convergence in antitrust enforcement.

A particular procedural issue was addressed by Bernd Meyring, namely the European Commission's use of interim measures in competition cases under Article 8 of Regulation No. 1/2003. He highlighted key examples and possible reasons for the European's infrequent use of interim measures and proposed conclusions on the instrument's suitability to prevent irreversible harm – ultimately agreeing that although interim measures do have a place, the lack of flexibility of the EU procedure in terms of procedural requirements merits further reflection, particularly with regard to situations of urgency.

Effective enforcement throughout the EU also raises the question of the organisation of competition authorities. Alexis Walckiers highlighted the stark differences of how investigations of alleged infringements are managed around the world and sought to address the issue that very little is actually known about how competition authorities should be organised. He discussed the significance of institutional design to enhance both efficiency and efficacy of competition authority investigations and examined various arguments in favour of independence of competition authorities vis-à-vis elected politicians whilst also, crucially, highlighting the associated constraints.

***

The second part of the conference was dedicated to the tentative areas for reform – labelled "Modernisation 2.0" – and the Outstanding Issues Beyond the Commission's Communication and Staff Working Paper.

Salvatore Rebecchini focused on the advocacy function of antitrust agencies and observed that despite recent international attention on advocacy, it has surprisingly been of little concern to the ECN thus far.

Advocacy in the ECN framework over the first ten years of application of Regulation No. 1/2003 are, in Mr Rebecchini's view, sporadic and insufficient and therefore offered three proposals to strengthen the role of the ECN as a network for advocacy, one of which is to establish an advocacy working group in the ECN, with very specific and detailed competences.

Finally, Mr Rebecchini drew from the wide experience of the Italian Competition Authority, which was granted a broad set of advocacy instruments to enhance and support pro-competitive initiatives of both a reactive and a pro-active nature, to conclude that the experience gathered in Italy could be a useful backdrop for the discussion which should take place at EU level for the adoption of a common advocacy tool-kit.

After having heard the point of view of agencies with Salvatore Rebecchini, Santiago Soldevila Fragoso shared his experience as a former judge of the General Court and, currently, as a judge of the Audencia Nacional in Madrid. He assessed the efficiency of judicial review at both national and EU levels. In doing so, Mr Soldevila Fragoso addressed the problem that the General Court faces, namely its significant backlog of cases, suggested a number of possible solutions, and considered their likely impact. Furthermore, the review process of some national courts regarding decisions of national competition authorities was evaluated, stressing the paradox that exists between the belief that the highest level of protection of fundamental rights is afforded by national courts rather than by EU courts and yet, depending on the jurisdiction, certain competition law cases can be decided in the absence of an oral hearing, which is, in Mr Soldevila Fragoso's view, a fundamental additional guarantee of defence.

Finally, another potential issue concerning convergence was raised by Gabriella Muscolo, namely the state of EU law in relation to the use of evidence in private enforcement, including discovery. It also addresses the issue of cooperation between national agencies and courts through amicus curiae and concludes with some reflections on judicial review in the Italian legal system.

The conference sparked a lively debate between all the speakers and the audience, a debate which Damien Gerard, the director of the GCLC, summarised in his concluding remarks that you will find at the end of this book.

KEYNOTE SPEECH

■

PHILIP LOWE[*]

President, Distinguished Guests, Ladies and Gentlemen,

May I express my thanks to GCLC for this invitation to speak and offer my congratulations to you for the timely organisation of this conference.

Could I first of all say that the views I express in this keynote address are personal and are meant in no way to reflect the position of the UK Competition and Markets Authority of which I am a non-executive Board Member. Similarly anything I may say must be interpreted in the context of my duty of discretion as a former official towards the European Commission and cannot be regarded in any way as either representing the position of the Commission or criticising it.

When only some days ago Jacques Bourgeois asked whether I would speak today on the how the Modernisation of the EC competition regime came about, I told him that there were a number of my former colleagues who would have far more legitimacy and authority in performing that task. To mention just a few (with apologies to others who also played an important role within and outside the Commission): Alex Schaub, Gianfranco Rocca, Jonathan Faull, Emil Paulis, Olivier Guersent. They all distinguished themselves in their efforts to create a new framework for the application of Articles 101 and 102 which would make European competition law enforcement and policy more efficient and more effective. In giving my own personal perspective on Modernisation, I must first of all pay tribute to their creativity, their personal commitment and above to their achievement which culminated in the adoption of Regulation 1/2003 and of the Guidance notes which accompanied it, as well as the creation of the European Competition Network. I am also sure that each one of them would

---

[*] Director general for Energy 2010-2014 and for Competition 2002-2010, European Commission.

have strong opinions on the issues which you will be discussing over the next two days: an assessment of the application of the Regulation in the last ten years and the ambitions which we should have for the European Competition law regime for the next ten years.

Successive Competition Commissioners also put their weight behind the negotiation, the adoption and the implementation on Regulation 1 and of subsequent additions: Mario Monti in particular played a crucial role, but under Neelie Kroes and Joaquin Almunia, several important instruments of application of 101 and 102, as well as the Directive on Damage Actions, have complemented the original texts.

Of course, in looking forward to a better European competition regime for the next two decades, in the present age of impatience for rapid results, we probably all agree with Thomas Jefferson when he said that he liked the dreams of the future better than the history of the past. However, we will arguably not make a success of the modernization of Modernisation unless we remember why Modernisation in 2003 and 2004 took place at all.

And, with apologies to those here who were at primary school at the time, that means looking back, not 10 years but 20, in 1994. Karel van Miert was then Competition Commissioner and Klaus Ehlermann was Director General. Economic and political conditions in Europe looked then a lot more favourable than today. Admittedly the debate around the Maastricht Treaty had given Europe's political elite the first warning of a lack of popular support for a Europe run by European institutions alone. But there was confidence around: the 1992 project of a Single European Market seemed to have been largely completed. Major Structural Funds programmes had been launched to help the poorer regions of Spain, Portugal, Greece and Ireland to catch up and to revitalize the declining industrial areas in the rest of Europe. Germany was reunified politically and increasingly economically. The preparations for a single currency were well underway.

Yet in many areas, European policies were not defined or developed to meet the challenges of governing a Europe which was increasingly integrated across frontiers and which was beginning to feel the impact of globalization: global markets, global media and communications, global movements of labour and capital. In addition, there were widely diverging views of what a European policy really was. In many capitals of Europe, both politicians and national administrations had the impression that Commission initiatives were simply designed to centralize more powers in its own hands at the expense of national institutions and agencies. They were not discouraged from this view by the many officials of the Commission who genuinely believed in a kind of zero-sum game in which by definition being more European meant being less national.

European competition policy was not excluded from this debate. After seventeen years of negotiation, national governments and agencies had finally agreed on the need for a European one-stop shop for control of mergers with more or less exclusive competence for the Commission above the turnover thresholds. But opinions were strongly divided on the efficiency and effectiveness of centralized powers in Brussels for other competition cases.

There was frankly deep suspicion of the Commission, with major discontent among national agencies, led by the Heads of the Bundeskartellamt and of the then DGCCRF in Paris, over the exclusive competence of the Commission to exempt agreements under 101(3). And from the point of view of effectiveness and efficiency, they were not alone in their criticism of the Commission. The notification of agreements to the Commission certainly gave parties temporary legal certainty at EC level and temporary immunity from prosecution of cases at national level. However in most cases, legal certainty was already provided by more than thirty years of European case law which an exemption decision from the Commission could do little to improve on. And the notification system led to an unmanageable backlog of cases which DG Competition (or DG IV as it was then known), even if it had obtained substantially increased resources, had no hope of clearing except by the legally dubious device of issuing so-called comfort letters to those transactions which it felt prima facie that it would not pursue. At the same time, in practice, the dominant criteria for treatment of cases were not associated with the likely economic harm of a conduct or agreement but with the longevity of the notification of an agreement or of the registration of a complaint and the likelihood of legal challenge. As a general rule, there was also no systematic economic assessment of a case, based on a clear geographic and product market definition and assessment of the market dynamics. And the results in terms of antitrust case work were modest and painfully slow.

In startling contrast, the new Merger Task Force appeared at least to be efficient-it respected short legal deadlines- and effective: it acted to prevent or modify mergers which were likely to reduce effective competition.

So in 1994, ten years before Modernisation, there were in effect two Commission Directorates general for Competition: The Merger Task Force and the rest. Andre Malraux once said that he loved Germany so much that he hoped there would always be two Germanies. His hopes were obviously dashed. However very few colleagues or commentators believed that

DG Competition could continue to live in this schizophrenia. Admittedly there were those who thought the schism should be put to an end immediately by abolishing the Merger Task Force! In their view this would at least prevent the drain of good colleagues from the rest of the DG to the MTF. But their solution did not resolve the fundamental issue as to how the European competition rules, alongside national rules, could be applied in a way which meant that antitrust harm would be the focus of attack and that as a result European markets would be more competitive in the interests of both consumers and business.

It was to this challenge that Karel van Miert, Klaus Ehlermann and their successors responded. And after many years of hard pounding, Regulation 1/2003 was adopted and the European Competition Network became a reality.

The principles at the basis of Regulation 1 were groundbreaking and, even now, their application outside the area of antitrust would arguably have positive and profound consequences for a wide range of European policies.

In the first place, preserving and promoting competitive markets in Europe is *not* a zero-sum game between the European and national level. There are some problems which are more effectively dealt with at a national or indeed regional level (centre of gravity of the issues in market terms, proximity of the agency to the markets and the facts, capacity to pursue the cases to successful conclusions and adopt appropriate sanctions and remedies...). On the other hand, there are other cases where the market definition is at least European if not global and/or where the issues and remedies should be applicable across several national jurisdictions.

Regulation 1 explicitly and sometimes implicitly recognises the principle of the authority 'best placed' to deal with a competition issue. Arguably the European Merger Regulation recognises the same thing, which is that the governance of Europe is necessarily something which should be achieved both through national action and action at European level. Both levels are vital for efficiency and effectiveness. And the national level has at least for the moment more potential to generate grass-roots support for competition policy action, in national and social media. As a result, as the Commission's Staff Working Document shows, the parallel application of EU competition rules, by the Commission and by national authorities and courts, has resulted in wider and more effective enforcement action.

In my view, the issue here is not of subsidiarity in the sense of certain competencies being exclusively at national level at others exclusively at European level. Many politicians and academics yearn for that kind of world where you can compartmentalise things at a particular jurisdictional level. Unfortunately economics and markets make it very difficult to do that. Sometimes problems are dealt with better at a national level even if they are common to several jurisdictions. At other times, it makes sense to mandate a supranational authority like the European Commission to pursue a case even though theoretically it could be dealt with in parallel by several national authorities. A lot therefore depends on the intelligence and common sense applied to the notion of which is the authority or authorities best placed to deal with a case.

The second most important principle behind Regulation 1 is that in most cases firms, together with their legal advisers, can well assess themselves whether a particular agreement or conduct is incompatible with EU competition law. They don't need the imprimatur of a Commission decision or a comfort letter to give them sufficient legal certainty. And as a result of not having to deal with a large volume of notifications, both the Commission and the national competition authorities can and should intervene where the likely harm to competition and to consumers is the greatest. As I will refer to later, there can be situations where more upfront legal certainty for parties is justified. But it doesn't make sense in the majority of situations. I think the ability of European competition authorities to devote more resources to tackling hardcore cartels – the most pernicious form of anticompetitive practice- and to the most harmful unilateral conduct cases, is largely due to the impact of Regulation 1.

Perhaps the third important principle underlying the Regulation was that of the independence of competition authorities from political and commercial influence and their capacity, with their own resources, to pursue investigations to a successful conclusion. These provisions of the Regulation have been a substantial support to the establishment of effective competition authorities in the newer Member States.

Finally, Regulation 1 opened the door for the first time to decisions which allow competition authorities to close cases on the basis of formal commitments provided by the parties. This has undoubtedly led to swifter and more effective resolution of issues where remedies for the future can make markets work better whereas a simple fine and cease and desist decision may not change anything.

Having said all this, having read and digested the Commission's assessment of the last ten years and the recommendations it makes for improvements, what should our ambitions be for the next ten years?

I would first of all congratulate the authors of the Commission's Report and Staff Working Document on a comprehensive, thorough and objective assessment of the experience so far and on their balanced and sober recommendations for the future.

But perhaps I could stray beyond the careful wording of the Commission documents. My personal view is that in the last ten years we have witnessed strong convergence in the substantive aims of both national and EU competition policies. Different traditions emphasise different aspects of our competition assessments, some on the dynamic of competition on the market, others on the impact on consumer welfare. The reality is that in most cases, the assessments carried out in different authorities have much in common, even if the proposed remedies differ. More could certainly be achieved through upstream discussion of issues between case teams and case managers before divergences have to be managetd at the most senior level. In the case of differences between national authorities on national cases, it is easy to suggest that the Commission should take over. But does it make sense for the Commission to be dealing with issues only because of different assessments at national level? Surely the Commission should only get involved where there is a genuine European-wide dimension to a case, at least in terms of precedent-setting. Ideally national authorities themselves should start off parallel cases by bringing their teams together to make sure the analysis and diagnosis of problems in each authority converge on the same results.

Perhaps the biggest challenge nevertheless relates to procedure. Having created a framework for parallel application of EU competition rules, by the Commission and national authorities, surely it's now time to see what progress can be made to create a genuinely European-wide competition regime. With respect to business, it would be a key element of best practice for Europe vis-à-vis the rest of the world. We have for example an ECN Model Leniency Regime. But you have to be a legal genius, with expert lawyers, and an expert tactician, to work out where to apply for what with potentially 28 different competition authorities in Europe. I know we should be aware of the idiosyncrasies of different national judicial systems. But do they make sense in terms of effectiveness and efficiency of law enforcement or indeed of defence of individual rights? In today's globalised and competitive world, the differences in national systems in Europe are a luxury we may no longer be able to afford.

Equally we know for some years now that some of our national jurisdictions believe anti-cartel enforcement is more effective when there are also sanctions, including criminal sanctions, against individuals. A considerable body of opinion believes that regimes of individual sanctions could live comfortably alongside the administrative sanctions against firms. Should we not be ambitious enough to say in more detail how this should work in practice?

Thirdly, we all know full well that the level of fines and other sanctions applied by different competition authorities in Europe varies widely. Is there any objective justification for these differences? I would suspect that as far as antitrust policy itself is concerned, these divergences could be removed, even if the general characteristics of national judicial systems justify some divergences.

Again on the different powers available to the Commission and national authorities to carry out investigations, including dawn raids, we hear on a periodic basis of stories about cooperation, or more usually lack of it, between different national competition authorities and courts. Can't we make some attempt to make things easy for investigators and also simpler and more transparent for parties?

With respect to the Commission itself, there are several areas where the experience of the last ten years could justify some adaptation to policy and practice. Having gained the benefits for Europe of a self-assessment system, it would surely be ill-advised to give into pressure for either the Commission or national authorities to provide 101(3) exemption decisions when requested on a general basis. That would be a step backwards into an antitrust world dominated by demands for legal certainty rather than by action against the most harmful anticompetitive practices. On the other hand, there are agreements relating to behaviour and structure where there is genuine uncertainty about the compatibility of the transaction or conduct with EU law. In those specific circumstances, it should be possible for the Commission to accede to a specific request, without the firms having to wait perhaps several years for an amendment to general guidance to the terms of a block exemption.

I believe too that the Commission could readily give more frequent and timely guidance to national courts in amicus briefs. National procedures should also explicitly allow for the Commission to submit its views on national investigations, as indeed national authorities do on Commission cases through the Advisory Committee. There is of course a resource issue for the Commission here. But the use of resources should be related to the overall enforcement priorities and submitting an amicus brief could well be the most effective way of contributing to those priorities in particular sectors and markets.

However, in terms of overall conclusions, I believe one can say with confidence that Regulation 1/2003 has been a salvation for competition policy in Europe. It united the Commission and the national authorities round common cause of preserving and promoting competitive markets in Europe. In terms of cooperation between authorities, it established the sound principle of identifying the authority which was best placed to handle a case and diffused a politically charged debate over the division of competences between the European and national level. It rescued DG Competition from the quagmire of binding but redundant notifications. It allowed all competition authorities to establish clear enforcement priorities and on this basis establish targeted programmes of enforcement action, especially in the fight against cartels.

But there is no room for complacency or pussyfooting around some of the things which could be done to maintain the EU's position as one of, if not the leading, antitrust jurisdictions in the world- transparent, uncomplicated and fair to business, but tough on anticompetitive agreements and conduct and friendly to justified complainants. As there is now a recognised role for authorities at the European and the national level, as well as strong convergence on the aims of antitrust action in Europe, it is time for a further effort towards procedures of European-wide application. The going will be tough, but as with Regulation 1 itself, the prize at the end will sbe worth it.

A very successful conference to all of you!

PL/06/11/14

I

PROCEDURAL CONVERGENCE IN ANTITRUST ENFORCEMENT – A PERSPECTIVE FROM THE INSIDE

PANEL SESSION ON PROCEDURAL CONVERGENCE

■

PHILIP MARSDEN

My role at the Competition and Markets Authority is as an Inquiry Chair, acting as a decision-maker on Phase 2 Merger inquiries, Market Investigation References, regulatory appeals and chairing Case Decision Groups in antitrust cases. I am not involved directly in investigations or policy-setting; that said, even so the following remarks are offered in my personal capacity. [1]

Introduction

Firstly, we should acknowledge how far we've come in 10 years in terms of reducing costs of divergence. Enforcement in the EU does look very different now compared to how it used to. The 2012 ECN reports on investigative and decision-making powers provide ample evidence of that. But they also show that significant differences remain. What are the implications of this?

The UK Government has been reviewing the "balance of competences" between the UK and EU. The paper on competition from earlier this year said that:

> "the evidence suggests strongly that a supranational EU competition regime with a central authority at its heart is vital to the realisation of the Single Market, to making markets work well and to minimising the burden on business. The system of shared competence for dealing with cases within the European Competition Network appears to work well, with cases generally being taken by the authority best placed to investigate and with consistent application of the rules across the EU encouraged".

---

[1] Thanks to Stephen Blake and Andrew Pickering for assistance in preparing these remarks.

And while the paper did note some concerns from stakeholders about divergent analyses in cases, procedural differences between NCAs weren't emphasised.

Nonetheless, the UK NCA – the Competition and Markets Authority (CMA) has supported the ECN Recommendations that Ailsa has referred to. We believe, as the Commission does, that effective enforcement needs authorities to have a full suite of powers. And we're lucky that we've been in the vanguard here, in terms of our domestic situation. The CMA has new powers such as the ability to apply fines for failure to comply with investigative measures (e.g. information requests), and a new compulsory interview power for CA98/TFEU cases.

I'll outline a couple of general thoughts on powers and procedures, before saying a few words on leniency in particular.

I think any work to bring about further convergence should still allow room for innovation and experimentation among national authorities. So there may be scope for a kind of middle ground between the status quo and complete harmonisation (which in any case isn't likely in the foreseeable future). One can envisage a kind of framework for the proper use of powers, yet without being too prescriptive.

One brief point I would like to make about national procedures is that, from my point of view, we could perhaps all do a little better at being transparent. One innovation we have recently made in the UK is to post case opening notices on our website. This give basic (admittedly sometimes quite limited) information on our open cases, including timescales. That's important for people to see what kind of caseload we have, and in which sectors, at the very least.

In terms of further work on the consistent application of the rules, I think it is interesting to assess the experience with soft convergence on powers. Some Recommendations have only been published for a year or two. As we know from the UK experience, reviews of national law and procedures come about less frequently than that, and they last longer. Have we given it enough time? That said – perhaps many – areas where convergence has not occurred have been because of national rules and legal traditions that go beyond competition law. That is not likely to change any time soon on the basis of an ECN Recommendation. Even so, I would be interested to get the Commission's view on whether more could be done with those Recommendations.

Leniency

We support the Commission's objective of ensuring that well-designed leniency programmes are in place in all Member States and significant progress has been made in this area, not least through the ECN.

On further leniency convergence – and, in particular, the call for a one-stop-shop – we are all familiar with the arguments for this. On the other hand, we need to recognise that without full EU harmonisation in the area of sanctions, as well as procedures, both of which present significant challenges, there will be limits to the extent that leniency convergence is possible. Moreover, whether such harmonisation will necessarily make for a stronger EU competition regime overall will obviously depend on what form it takes. In the case of the CMA, a key concern will be to ensure that the effectiveness of the UK criminal cartel regime is preserved.

There are a number of aspects to this. A key issue for any jurisdiction that provides for sanctions against individuals as well as undertakings will be to ensure that the two complement and support each other, or at least do not undermine each other. In particular, for leniency to be effective, the incentives for businesses and their employees to come forward and report cartel conduct need to be as aligned as possible. This is especially so where – as in the UK – individuals may be prosecuted criminally. Where the leniency policy operates in such a way that the incentives of individuals and their employers are aligned, securing immunity for individual employees can operate as a strong additional incentive to come forward. On the other hand, where individual immunity is not available (or cannot be guaranteed with a sufficient degree of certainty) the existence of individual sanctions can operate as a disincentive for undertakings to come forward and thus undermine the effectiveness of the regime overall.

As we know, another key ingredient for an effective leniency regime is to ensure maximum upfront certainty for applicants, particularly where there is no prior investigation. This applies equally (if not more so) to individual sanctions as to corporate sanctions and needs to be built into the design of the individual sanctions regime from the outset.

In international cases, leniency incentives also need to be aligned not only as between businesses and their employees, but also – so far as possible – across jurisdictions. This interdependence of leniency programmes means that an ineffective leniency regime in one jurisdiction can affect the leniency regime of another, hence the importance which the CMA places on working with other agencies – not only within the ECN but also globally, such as through the OECD and ICN.

This interdependence – in particular, within the ECN – is also why the CMA's leniency policy sets out in some detail how the policy interacts with that of the European Commission and why applicants in cartel cases involving the UK will always be advised to consider applying to the CMA. It is also why in parallel leniency cases the CMA recognises (and accepts) the need to work with the Commission and other relevant jurisdictions to help resolve any practical difficulties that may arise from differences between the respective regimes.

At the same time, however, we cannot avoid the fact that the overriding purpose of any leniency programme is to enable the competition authority to take effective enforcement action. What this requires will inevitably vary from jurisdiction to jurisdiction. In the case of the UK, one consequence of the criminal regime is the expectations the CMA places on leniency applicants and their advisors in relation to the approach to evidence and the conduct of internal investigations. This is set out in some detail in the CMA's guidance and is another key aspect of the CMA's leniency policy, which would need to be preserved.

Before I move on from leniency – and I know this is something Mr Prieto Kessler will return to later – it is, of course, important to remember that leniency is not the only source of cases. Indeed, almost half of new cartel investigations opened in the UK since 2010 have been intelligence led. This is also an area in which we are investing in further, including through the appointment of a Director of Intelligence to head our cartels intelligence function, which we hope to be able to announce shortly. So, even without leniency, the risk of detection in the UK is, I would suggest, higher than ever and increasing. That itself should be an important incentive for businesses to come forward and apply for immunity while it is still available.

Independence

It's right that if organisations are enforcing EU law, the Commission should be able to intervene to make sure EU law isn't being misused. That said, independence is not only about rules and legislation. It's also about what you do (or indeed don't do) on a day to day basis. And I think the Commission has recognised that. It's not always going to be obvious that one way of setting up an NCA guarantees independence where another doesn't. So I think it's hard to legislate for independence (though that is not to say that legislative efforts wouldn't help). We should also be careful to ensure that efforts to secure independence don't conflict with measures to preserve accountability. In the UK, the CMA has a performance management framework agreed with government, which designed to ensure we are accountable.[2] Does that mean we're not independent? I don't think so. Adam Jasser will speak more about that later and it will be particularly interesting to get a Polish perspective on this.

Serious thought will also be needed as to the way all these ideas could be implemented – and particularly as to how to avoid the process losing focus as stakeholders bring up every grievance they have with the status quo. (Or, to be provocative, would that be a good thing? Is a wider review required? Or indeed inevitable?). In any case, we cannot prejudge the Commissioner's own take on all of this.

While I'm not here to speak for the CMA per se, what I'm going to say now is very much with my academic hat on.

Transparency

There are different substantive approaches in different Member States on various practices, including RPM and fidelity rebates, for example. This is natural, particularly in markets with different economic priors, structures and enforcement priorities and mechanisms. There is increasing pressure to understand the rationale for these differences, though, and where this is still unclear, I would like to urge more transparency particularly with respect to providing clear reasoning in non-infringement, no-grounds for action and commitment decisions. The reasons for this are three: first, though it might not be a concern in some jurisdictions, it remains the case that in others there might be a suspicion that a case has been closed down due to political pressure. Providing clear reasoning will shine a light on and thereby, hopefully, rule out or at least deter this. Second, providing more reasoning would help learning among authorities and help develop a competition of ideas and methods, and thus a natural movement towards

---

[2] The Performance Framework sets out the performance the Government expects from the CMA and describes how the CMA will fulfil the performance reporting requirements of the Act. The CMA Board is accountable for the success of the CMA as a whole and the delivery of the objectives set out in the Performance Framework. The CMA must report annually on a number of benchmarks, including: (a) the delivery of a target of direct financial benefits to consumers of at least ten times its relevant costs to the taxpayer (measured over a rolling three-year period); (b) the ratio of direct financial benefits to consumers and costs for its principal tools; (c) its assessment of wider benefits of its work, for example on growth, business and consumer confidence in markets, compliance with competition law and deterrence of anticompetitive behaviour.

more informed divergence and possibly greater convergence. Thirdly, more reasoning is necessary – particularly where enforcement approaches are unclear or diverge – to provide guidance to industry on what is and isn't prohibited, thus deterring conduct that crosses the line, but equally not chilling pro-competitive business conduct that is not problematic from a competition law perspective.

Case allocation

Seems to becoming more important lately. Case allocation generally works well – whether the Commission taking a case or national authorities (either individually or in concert – but perhaps the efficiency of the case allocation system can be improved further, with better prioritisation and early-stage coordination.

There is no formal mechanism which would allow multiple NCAs which are investigating similar antitrust issues to petition for the Commission to take the case from them. This stands in contrast to arrangements under the EUMR. There may be circumstances in which NCAs feel the Commission is better placed to take a case forward, and where multiple cases in different Member States are an unduly burdensome means of addressing a competition problem. There can be clear efficiency reasons for the Commission to take on cases like this – both in terms of avoiding potential duplication among NCAs and for the parties involved to the investigations – those under investigation, but also third parties.

While NCAs may provide support to the Commission in carrying out inspections and may also cooperate with other NCAs' investigations, it could also be beneficial to examine means by which staff could be reallocated between authorities along with cases, or to remain involved in cases which are taken on elsewhere. This could allow for the creation of a multinational 'task force' for cases affecting several national markets and where expertise is spread among different NCAs.

And more could be done to ensure that enforcement is prioritised effectively among NCAs and DG Comp. While of course it is not the intention to seek to align NCAs' priorities, it is good to have constructive dialogue between partners in the EU competition system, and further exchanges would be informative and could help avoid duplication. This could apply both to antitrust enforcement and to market studies and sector inquiries, the latter where the UK has a strong history and where other countries are becoming more active.

POWER TO SET ENFORCEMENT PRIORITIES [1]

■

LAURENCE IDOT[*]

1. The starting point of this presentation can be found in the last report made in July 2014 by the Commission for the 10th anniversary of Regulation 1/2003.[2]

In the second *Staff Working Document,*[3] more specifically in the part 3 on convergence of procedures, it is said: "divergence subsists for some fundamental questions, e.g. whether competition authorities have the power to set priorities".[4]

Later on, it is asserted:

"The following aspects have been identified within the *European Competition Network* (hereinafter, ECN) as forming key components of the toolbox that authorities should have at their disposal:

a. Priority setting: there is a need for further convergence on the ability of the authorities to set priorities in the exercise of their tasks and maximise administrative efficiency when choosing which cases to pursue. Progress has been made in this regard in Greece and Portugal, where the NCAs are now able to set their priorities and to reject complaints without the need for a detailed investigation on substance. However, some NCAs still have a legal duty to consider all complaints and requests for interim measures received. The ECN Recommendation on the power to set priorities advocates for authorities to have greater flexibility to choose which cases to investigate".[5]

---

[1] All expressed views are purely personal. The oral style of the presentation has been kept.
[*] Professor, University Panthéon-Assas (Paris II), Member of the College, Autorité de la Concurrence (Fr).
[2] Commission, Communication to the European Parliament and the Council, "Ten Years of Antitrust Enforcement under Regulation 1/2003: Achievements and Future Perspectives", COM(2014) 453, {SWD(2014) 230}, 9 July 2014.
[3] Commission, "Enhancing competition enforcement by the Member States' competition authorities: institutional and procedural issues", SWD(2014) 231/2.
[4] *Idem,* pt 45.
[5] *Idem,* pt 59.

Thus, the Commission confirms in its report the conclusions made previously in December 2013, when the ECN adopted a recommendation on the power to set priorities[6] (hereinafter, *ECN Recommendation*).

2. More broadly, prioritisation is a general concern within the international organisations that work on competition policy and agency effectiveness such as OECD,[7] UNCTAD,[8] ICN.[9] At the same time, excellent studies have already been written on the topic.[10]

These works demonstrate that there is a clear link between the power to set priorities and Competition Authorities' discretion. However, the concept of discretion is broader.[11] First, it may apply to the qualification of conducts.[12] Second, even if it is limited to enforcement aspects, discretion may apply at different stages of the proceedings.[13]

3. In the enforcement context, the *ECN recommendation* explains that the notion of priority setting may be understood in two ways.[14]

Priority setting may be understood at a general level in a policy perspective. In this context, priority setting means the ability of NCAs to prioritise

---

[6] ECN Recommendation on the power to set priorities, available: http://ec.europa.eu/competition/ecn/recommendation_priority_09122013_en.pdf.

[7] See, for instance, OECD, Competition Committee, "Evaluation of the Actions and Resources of the Competition Authorities", 2005.

[8] UNCTAD, Intergovernmental Group of Experts on Competition Law and Policy 13th Session, 8 to 10 July 2013, Geneva, "Priority setting and resource allocation as a tool for agency effectiveness", with the presentation of F. Jenny, "Priority setting and discretionary powers of competition authorities", available: http://unctad.org/meetings/en/Presentation/IGE2013_PRESPrior_Jenny_en.pdf.

[9] ICN, see the works of the subgroup, Agency Effectiveness; chapter I of the Competition Agency Practice Manual, "Strategic Planning and Prioritisation", March 2010, available: http://www.internationalcompetitionnetwork.org/uploads/library/doc744.pdf.

[10] N. Petit, "How much discretion do, and should, competition authorities enjoy in the course of their enforcement activities? A multi-jurisdictional assessment", general report made for the LIDC Vienna Congress, October 2009, available, *Concurrences*, No. 1-2010, pp. 44-62; W. Wils, "Discretion and Prioritisation in Public Antitrust Enforcement", *World Competition*, vol. 34, No. 3, September 2011, http://ssrn.com/author=456087.

[11] W. Wils, *op. cit.*

[12] W. Wils, *op. cit.* The discretion of the authority varies according to the vagueness of the applicable rules. It is also submitted to the control of the courts. It may be argued that the Commission communication on Article 102 TFUE ("Guidance on the Commission's enforcement priorities in applying Article 82 of the EC Treaty to abusive exclusionary conduct by dominant undertakings", *OJEU*, 2009, C 45) is an illustration of this concept of "discretion" applied to substantive issues. It also illustrates that this kind of discretion is subject to the control of the Court.

[13] For instance, N. Petit demonstrated that CAs may be entitled to make choices at different levels of the proceeding: detection of infringement, selection of enforcement targets, initiation of infringement proceedings, outcome of the case.

[14] *Supra* note, see pt 2.

and plan their work, to formulate strategic plans, decisions on the allocation of resources across all areas of responsibility. In other words, it may be defined as a "strategy of setting general priorities". [15]

Priority setting can also be given a more specific connotation. In this second meaning, it refers to the discretion of NCAs to initiate investigations and start proceedings in relation to individual cases. It may be defined as "individual case priority setting".

4. Considering the general subject matter of this colloquium, we will understand the topic only in relation with the second meaning and we will focus on the assertion of the Commission that: *"there is a need for further convergence on the ability of the authorities to set priorities when choosing which cases to pursue"*.

It is generally assumed that such a system enables competition authorities to be more efficient. It might have been useful to study the veracity of this assertion. However these points have already be discussed in the previously mentioned works [16] and the data are now well known.

For the 10th anniversary of Regulation 1/2003, we will only focus on the need for further convergence. Unlike many authorities on the subject, and with all due respect, I confess that I do not agree on the need for further convergence for the following reasons. Some doubts may be expressed both on the merits of the diagnosis (I) and on the adequacy of the remedies (II).

I. Is the diagnosis right?

5. Convergence on prioritisation is justified if two conditions are met: the purported divergences are real (A) and these divergences have a significant impact on the functioning of the network (B).

A. Reality of divergences?

6. Different distinctions are usually made, but they do not reflect the reality of national laws.

---

[15] Some NCAs publically assert these general priorities at the end of the year for the coming year. It's a kind of agenda. See, for instance, The Dutch and the Portuguese Authorities.

[16] See, for instance, W. Wils, *supra*, sp. part. V, the arguments in favour of prioritisation and prioritisation risks.

A first distinction needs to be introduced in the discussion. Priority setting in individual cases has two aspects: a positive one and a negative one.

7. The positive aspect of priority setting is the ability of a competition authority to take action *ex officio* with regard to identified cases. It is true that it is a key aspect of the ability of NCAs to set priorities. No surprisingly the importance of this power was acknowledged in Regulation 1/2003. Article 5 underlines the possibility for NCAs to act on their own initiative. To the best of my knowledge, no problem has been identified within the network. All NCAs are entitled to act *ex officio*. However, this issue is not only a legal one and has mainly practical aspects. The competition authority needs to have sufficient human and material means to achieve its tasks.

The French example before the 2008 reform is interesting. In France, when it was created by the ordinance of 1st December 1986, the former Competition Council received the power to act *ex officio*.[17] However, for years, this right was rarely used, since the Council did not have its own investigation services to undertake inquiries, which were made by the services of the ministry of economy, the DGCCRF. It mainly dealt with the cases transmitted by the DGCCRF and by complainants.[18] The entry into force of Regulation 1/2003 began to modify the situation since the Competition Council opened cases *ex officio* following leniency applications, which were made both before the Commission and the NCAs that could intervene.[19] However the main change occurred after the 2008 reform when the new *Autorité de la concurrence* obtained the legal and human means to undertake its own inquiries.[20] Furthermore, due to a system of preliminary exchanges between the DGCCRF and the General Rapporteur of the *Autorité de la concurrence*,[21] the ministry of economy progressively ceased to introduce cases.[22]

---

[17] Ord. 1st Dec. 1986, Art. 11 became Commerce code (hereinafter, Com. C.), Art. L 462-5.

[18] The relations between the different kinds of opening the cases (*ex officio*/ministry of economy/complainants) are the following: 1992: 0/50/48; 1993: 2/43/46; 1994: 1/27/51; 1995: 2/41/61; 1996: 4/35/58; 1997: 4/26/51; 1998: 3/30/74; 1999: 7/24/51; 2000: 5/20/61; 2001: 4/16/59; 2002: 5/11/42; 2003: 2/16/41; 2004: 6/10/32; 2005: 9/15/32; 2006: 9/17/34; 2007: 3/13/41; 2008: 6/6/37.

[19] The leniency proceeding was introduced in French law by the so-called "NRE" law of 15 May 2001, but it did not work before the entry into force of the Regulation 1/2003 (Com. C, Art. L 464-2-IV).

[20] For a general presentation of the reform, see *Autorité de la concurrence*, Annual Report, 2008.

[21] Com. C., Art. L 450-5.

[22] The reform made by the law of 4 August 2008 entered into force in March 2009. The repartition between different types of authority referral is the following: 2009: 8/4/42; 2010: 13/2/44; 2011: 12/0/28; 2012:5/0/26; 2013: 3/0/20.

8. Priority setting also has a negative aspect. It is the possibility to reject complaints in relation to cases that are not deemed a priority by the Authority. This issue is more difficult to deal with. In EU law, since the *GEMA* decision of the Court of Justice[23] and subsequent case law of the Court of First Instance,[24] it is the rule for the Commission.[25] However this solution is not general.

9. It leads to the second distinction. It is recognized that there are mainly two systems within the ECN members.[26]

The first one may be called a prioritisation-based system. It seems to be applied mainly in Belgium, Ireland, Germany, Netherlands, Sweden, United Kingdom.[27] It is opposed to a system based on the legality principle, which triggers a legal duty to consider all complaints. Such a system is adopted in France and Italy.

In its report, the Commission is clearly in favour of the first system. It is said:

"*Progress* has been made in this regard in Greece and Portugal, where the NCAs are now able to set their priorities and to reject complaints without the need for a detailed investigation on substance".[28]

10. Such a binary classification is too simple. The reality is much more diversified. As it is acknowledged in the ECN recommendation, there are great differences between the NCAs that apply the first system.[29]

They may concern the procedural treatment of the complaint. Complaints are sometimes only a source of information and the NCA initiates the case only on an *ex officio* basis. In other jurisdictions, the Authorities have to address complaints, but they have the possibility to decide not to conduct an in-depth investigation. In such a situation, the methods of closing a case

---

[23] CJEC, 18 October 1979, 125/78, ECR-3174.

[24] In the nineties, the Court of First Instance played a decisive role to build a specific regime of complaints. See, J.-B. BLAISE and L. IDOT, "La jurisprudence du Tribunal de première instance en matière de concurrence", *Revue du marché unique commun et de l'Union européenne*, 1995, pp. 109-126.

[25] See, Commission Notice on the handling of complaints by the Commission under Articles 81 and 82 of the EC Treaty, *OJEU*, 27 April 2004, No. C 101/65 ; Commission notice on best practices for the conduct of proceedings concerning Articles 101 and 102 TFEU, *OJEU*, 20 October 2011, No. C 308, sp. Chap. 5, pts 134-141.

[26] ECN Recommendation, pt 3.

[27] See also, in the Czech Republic (ECN Brief, 1/2013), Cyprus.

[28] SWD, *op. cit.*, pt 59.

[29] ECN Recommendation, *op. cit.*, pt 5.

on priority grounds differ and range from informal means, such as informal letters, which are not judicially reviewable, to formal decisions.[30]

Other divergences concern the criteria that are used to decide whether to move forward with a case or not, and transparency of these criteria. Several jurisdictions have adopted prioritisation principles. In the United Kingdom, the *Office of Fair Trading* was the first one to set the example in 2008 and the new *Competition Markets Authority* follows the same line.[31] For instance, such principles have also been adopted in 2010 by the Swedish CA[32] and the Greek one,[33] in 2011 by the Irish CA,[34] in 2012 by the Dutch one.[35]

11. National systems based upon the legality principle also present differences which might not be visible at first glance. Each national system has its specificity and should be looked at in its entirety.

The French system is a good example. The FCA has the duty to reach a formal decision on each complaint.[36] The rule was not modified in 2008[37] but major changes occurred on other points. Different tools to deal with minor infringements exist. In addition to the French equivalent of the *de minimis rule*,[38] which doesn't work, there is a specific regime for local anticompetitive conducts, which are dealt with by the Ministry of Economy under a settlement procedure.[39] Furthermore, in the case of ordinary proceedings before the FCA, two filters may be used. The first filter covers

---

[30] That's the rule for the Commission since the *Guérin* case (C-282/95 P, ECR 2007-I-1503; ECLI:EU:C:1997:159).

[31] Competition and Markets Authority (UK), Prioritisation principles for the CMA, April 2014, CMA 16.

[32] Swedish Competition Authority (Konkurrensverket), 4 January 2010, Policy for prioritization of competition and procurement cases ("Konkurrensverkets policy för prioritering av konkurrens- och upphandlingsfrågor"), Doc. No. 475/2009. See, S. NORDIN, e-Competitions, No. 30710, www.concurrences.com.

[33] Hellenic Competition Commission (Elliniki Epitropi Antagonismou), 12 January 2010, Notice on Enforcement Priorities. See, I. KOUNIAKI, e-Competitions, No. 34260, www.concurrences.com.

[34] Irish Competition Authority, Project Selection and Prioritisation Principles, July 2011.

[35] NMa, 14 February 2012, Prioritization guidelines, ECN Brief and e-Competitions, No. 46878, www.concurrences.com.

[36] The word "complaint" is not used in French law. The legal term is "saisine". This choice is not neutral, since, if the referral is admissible, its author becomes a party to the proceedings.

[37] A case can now be closed, but only following an *ex officio* opening. Com. C., Art. L 462-8, al. 5.

[38] Com. C., Art. L 464-6-1 and L 464-6-2. The rule was introduced by an ordinance in March 2004.

[39] Com. C., Art. L 464-9. This system is presently under review. Anyway it is outside the scope of the ECN since it only concerns practices that do not affect trade between MS. However, in recent cases, the interpretation of this condition has been contested.

admissibility (standing, time of limitations, jurisdiction).[40] A second filter can be used in an efficient way to the extent that the complaint may be rejected for lack of sufficient elements to prove the anticompetitive conduct.[41] During the Council's first years of activity, there were a lot of repetitive complaints, but the statistics from more recent years demonstrate that this is no longer the case.[42]

In the nineties, some comparative analyses were made between the French system and the procedural treatment of complaints by the European Commission.[43] The conclusion was clear. In the end, a great convergence may be observed as far as concrete results are concerned. The EU specific proceeding to handle complaints[44] is more complex: two rounds of exchanges, instead one in French Law; a final decision which is more detailed since the judicial control is more acute. The main difference concerns the grounds which may be invoked to reject the complaint. Under French law, they are always objective, such as time limitations, lack of jurisdiction, lack of proofs... Unlike the Commission, the FCA cannot rely on "subjective" grounds such as the lack of Community interest.

12. The first conclusion is clear. A serious comparative analysis of different systems should be carried out before going further. So far, it does not exist. Furthermore, the negative impact of these divergences on the functioning of the network has not been established.

B. What is the impact of these divergences on the functioning of the network?

13. According to the recommendation: "further convergence on the ability of the Authorities to set priorities would help enhance effectiveness and efficiency in the enforcement of competition rules..." If one looks at the past ten years, this assertion is not supported by available data.

---

[40] Com. C., Art. L 462-8, al. 1.
[41] Com. C., Art. L 462-8, al. 2.
[42] See *supra* the statistics notes 18 and 22.
[43] L. Idot, "La plainte en droit de la concurrence. Opposition ou convergence du droit communautaire et du droit français", in *Mélanges en l'honneur de Louis Boyer*, Toulouse, Presses de l'Université des Sciences sociales de Toulouse, pp. 255-281; D. Barthe, *La situation des victimes de pratiques anticoncurrentielles devant les autorités de concurrence communautaire et française*, (Ph. D, Paris I), Aix-en-Provence, PUAM, 2000.
[44] See the notice, *op. cit.*, note 23.

14. The first observation cannot be discussed. It is not confirmed by the statistics.[45]

Cases per Member State:		
Member State	New case investigations	Envisaged case decisions (Art. 11(4) of Reg. 1/2003)
Austria	43	14
Belgium	48	13
Bulgaria	19	6
Croatia	2	
Cyprus	11	5
Czech Republic	15	9
Denmark	74	45
Germany	175	104
Greece	45	41
Estonia	7	3
Finland	26	11
France	228	109
Hungary	99	30
Ireland	18	2
Italy	117	100
Latvia	19	5
Lithuania	22	20
Luxembourg	10	5
Malta	5	3
The Netherlands	96	48
Poland	29	13
Portugal	60	17
Romania	46	29
Slovakia	19	17
Slovenia	30	28
Spain	119	91
Sweden	53	21
United Kingdom	69	16

If you take into consideration the right-hand column with the envisaged decisions, two NCAs with opposite systems are on top: the French authority on one side (109 envisaged decisions); the German one on the other (104 envisaged decisions). At the bottom of the list of the big Member States, the British Authority, which has the most marked system of prioritisation, can be found (only 16 envisaged decisions), widely outstripped by NCAs of smaller Member States such as the Dutch one (48 envisaged decisions), the Danish one (45 envisaged decisions).

---

[45] Available on the website of the DG comp. 1st May 2004 – 31st December 2014: http://ec.europa.eu/competition/ecn/statistics.html.

15. Of course, a merely quantitative perspective is of limited interest and it is necessary to go further and to introduce a qualitative approach, taking into consideration the French results. Its activity over the last decade enables us to draw four conclusions.[46]

First, the French practice is quite diversified. The Authority has not only dealt with cartels,[47] but has also adopted a lot of decisions both on vertical restraints[48] and on abuses of dominant positions.[49] More interestingly, some decisions on horizontal agreements other than cartels have also been taken.[50]

Second, many interesting decisions – either prohibition decisions or commitment decisions – have been adopted following complaints. A list, which only covers the year 2014, is enclosed.[51]

Third, the French CA was the first one to deal with many new topics, both jurisdictional and substantive. The preliminary requirement of an effect on trade between Member States was explained in the specific context of

---

[46] See the general annual reports available on the website, with a synthesis both in French and in English (http://www.autoritedelaconcurrence.fr/user/standard.php?id_rub=15). Many statistics may be found in the first part ("Rapport d'activité") following by a presentation of the cases in the third part ("Pratique de l'Autorité de la concurrence").

[47] See for instance, the list of decisions following leniency applications (http://www.autoritedelaconcurrence.fr/user/standard.php?id_rub=292&id_article=1004). Among the most important ones, see, dec. 11-D-17 (detergents; with a parallel case before the Commission), dec. 12-D-09 (flours; with parallel cases before the German and the Belgian Authority), dec. 13-D-12 (commodity chemicals), dec. 14-D-19 (home and personal care products).

[48] L. IDOT, "La pratique de l'Autorité française concurrence en matière de relations verticales ", *Revista Concorrencia e Regulaçao*, 2010/4, pp. 139-168 and *Concurrences*, No. 2010/4, Art. No. 52908, www.concurrences.com.

[49] For the action of the Authority in the network industries, L. IDOT, "L'autorité de la concurrence, régulateur des industries de réseaux?", in *Mélanges en l'honneur de D. Tricot*, Paris, Ed. Dalloz/Litec, 2011, pp. 183-206, "La contribution des autorités de concurrence à la politique de l'énergie de l'Union européenne", *Concurrences*, No. 2011/4, Art. No. 35609, pp. 66-79.

[50] See, for instance, the Expédia case, dec. 09-D-06 (origine of the referral: complaint); Cass. Com., 10 May 2011 (preliminary ruling to the Court of Justice); CJEU, 26 December 2012, C-226/11, ECLI:EU:C:2012:795; and following this decision Cass. Com., 16 April 2013 (all decisions available, http://www.autoritedelaconcurrence.fr/user/avisdec.php?numero=09-D-06); the digital system for processing checks, dec. 10-D-28, C. Appeals Paris, 23 February 2012 (available with the decision in English, http://www.autoritedelaconcurrence.fr/user/avisdec.php?numero=10D28#recours).

[51] *Prohibition decisions:* 15-D-01, TDF (exclusionary practices), 14-D-10, SNCF (abuses in the sale of train tickets); 14-D-06, Cegedim (abusive refusal to sell a database); 14-D-05, SFR (price discrimination between on net calls and off net calls); 14-D-02, Groupe Amaury (exclusion of a new entrant in the sports press). *Commitment decisions:* 14-D-11, commitments from SNCF allowing travel agencies to compete on an equal footing with voyages-sncf. com; 14-D-09, commitments from Nespresso to lift barriers to entry for othercoffee capsule makers; 14-D-04, commitment from the PMU, which will separate its online horserace betting activity from its network of points of sale under monopoly.

overseas territories.[52] On the substantive issues, it is possible to mention, for Article 101 TFEU, the scope of *de minimis* rule in the *Expédia* case, the relation between selective distribution and Internet in the *Pierre Fabre* case,[53] for Article 102 TFEU, peering agreements in the telecoms field...[54] Furthermore, it is the only authority, to the best of my knowledge, which has discussed the application of Article 101, § 3, TFEU.[55]

Fourth, it has not prevented the FCA to have a proactive attitude in some important fields, like payment systems,[56] sales on Internet,[57] generics,[58] and electronic communications...[59]

16. The second conclusion is clear. The negative impact of the so-called "legality principle" on the functioning of the network has not been demonstrated. A thorough study of the French practice demonstrates exactly the contrary. The major role of the French Competition Authority in the efficiency of the ECN cannot be denied. Since the diagnosis is debatable, it is possible to have some doubts about the adequacy of the remedies.

II. Are the contemplated remedies suitable?

17. So far, guiadance both on the principle (A) and on the implementation of prioritisation (B) may be found in the *ECN recommendation.*

---

[52] FCA, dec. 08-D-30, supply of kerosene La Réunion, Cass. Com., 1st March 2011, (http://www. autoritedelaconcurrence.fr/user/avisdec.php?numero=08D30); dec. 09-D-36, Orange Caraïbe, (origin of the referral, complaint), with an intervention of the Commission as *amicus curiae* based on art. 15, § 3, Regulation 1/2003, 13 October 2011, Cass. Com., 13 January 2012 (http://www.autoritedelaconcurrence.fr/user/avisdec.php?numero=09D36).

[53] See the famous *Pierre Fabre* case, FCA, dec. 08-D-25, C. Appeals Paris, 29 October 2009, preliminary ruling, CJEU, 13 October 2011, C-439/09, ECR 2011 I-09419, ECLI:EU:C:2011:649, and following the décision, C. Appeals Paris, 31 January 2013 (http://www.autoritedelaconcurrence.fr/user/avisdec.php?numero=08-D-25); *adde*, E. Combe, L. Idot and P. Rey, "Les nouvelles pratiques commerciales et la vente en ligne", *Concurrences*, No. 2013/4, Art. No. 57662, www.concurrences.com.

[54] FCA, dec. 12-D-18, Internet Traffic- Peering agreements, and C. Appeals Paris, 19 December 2013 (available with full text in English, http://www.autoritedelaconcurrence.fr/user/avisdec.php?numero=12-D-18).

[55] See the *Pierre Fabre* case and the *digital systems for checks* case, *op. cit.*, notes 45 and 46.

[56] See, the most commitment decisions, 13-D-17, *MasterCard*, and 13-D-18, *Visa*.

[57] See the joint action on parity clauses, market test 15 December 2014.

[58] FCA, dec. 13-D-11, *Sanofi-Aventis* (confimed by C. Appeals Paris, 18 December 2014; available, http://www.autoritedelaconcurrence.fr/user/avisdec.php?numero=13-D-11), dec. 13-D-21, *Schering Plough* (http://www.autoritedelaconcurrence.fr/user/avisdec.php?numero=13-D-21).

[59] L. Idot, "How has Regulation 1/2003 affected the role and work of national competition authorities? The French example", Mannheim, 7 juin 2013, NZart. 2014/1, pp. 12-17 and *Concurrences*, No. 2014/4, Art. No. 66394, www.concurrences.com.

A. Generalisation of a prioritisation system?

18. If, in the future, provisions implementing a prioritisation system are introduced in a regulation n° 1/2003 bis, both positive priority and negative priority should be covered.

19. As far as **positive priority** is concerned, a consensus seems to exist on the need for any NCA to be entitled to act *ex officio*. The ECN recommendation is quite clear.[60] However, there are two serious gaps in the text.

20. First, when a CA also has an advisory role and may deliver general opinions on competition issues, it is important to give it the power to act *ex officio* not only to deal with individual cases, but also to adopt general opinions. The French example is again interesting. The former *Competition Council* was entitled to deliver general opinions in two different contexts and a distinction was made between "facultative consultations" and "compulsory consultations".[61] These provisions remain in force, but since the 2008 reform, the new *Autorité de la concurrence* "may take the initiative to give an opinion on all questions concerning competition".[62] It has been justified in the following terms:

> *"The reform has granted the Authority the power to issue, at its own initiative, opinions concerning the competitive functioning of markets. Acting as an 'advocate of competition', it may, whenever it deems appropriate, express the point of view of a competition expert. It has the possibility, for example, to contribute to drawing up of legal texts or, furthermore, to recommending measures or actions in order to improve the competitive functioning of markets. This new possibility is highly important, since it will allow the new Authority to develop 'competition pedagogy' in order to educate public and economic players about the importance of competition. Hence, the Authority will be in a position to advise and to warn, in addition to its existing repressive mission, which it will, of course, continue to exercise".[63]*

---

[60] *Op. cit.*, pt 5 (i).
[61] Com. C., Art. L 462-1 and L 462-2.
[62] Com. C., Art. L 462-4.
[63] Presentation of the 2008 reform on the website of the FCA, http://www.autoritedelaconcurrence.fr/user/standard.php?id_rub=317.

Five years later, it is possible to say that it is one of the most efficient tools that can be used in order to adopt a proactive competition policy. So far, the Competition Authority has used this power nine times.[64]

21. The second gap covers interim measures. The French experience shows that they are a very useful tool. Many issues have been solved through this proceeding, which is always linked to a main request on the merits.[65] Very often, tt has enabled the Competition authority to intervene in network industries to solve crucial issues in decisive moments, like the launch of ADSL,[66] the development of internet-TV,[67] or the opening to competition in energy markets.[68] The decisions, on the distribution of the I-Phone,[69] adopted just before Christmas 2008, or in the field of broadcasting rights,[70] are also famous. There is an average of two positive decisions per year.[71]

However, there is also a paradox. The Authority has to deal with all requests for interim measures. In the past, this led to excessive workloads for the Authority.[72] Some lawyers used this proceeding to put the file on the top, but some pragmatic filters have been introduced and it is no longer an issue. On the other hand, unlike the Commission, the FCA cannot take interim measures *ex officio*, which makes no sense.

22. On **negative priority and the assessment of complaints,** I have to confess that I changed my mind after the 2008 reform. Before the reform, I was clearly in favour of the prioritisation system, but I am now more reluctant, both for legal and sociological reasons.

---

[64] Opinions 14-A-05, transport between regions by bus (dec. 13 SOA 02); 13-A-24, distribution of drugs in town (dec. 13 SOA 01); 13-A-21, vehicle repair and maintenance sector (dec. 11 SOA 01) ; 13-A-20, e-Commerce (dec. 11 SOA 02); 11-A-02, online betting and gambling (dec. 10 SOA 03); 10-A-26, retail in the food sector (dec. 10 SOA 01); 10-A-25, category management (dec. 10 SOA 02); 10-A-13, convergence between fixed lines and mobiles(dec. 09 SOA 02); 09-A-55, train stations, intermodality and competition in transportation (dec. 09 SOA 01). All opinions are available on the website and may be found through the search engine: http://www.autoritedelaconcurrence.fr/activites/avis/rech_avis.php.

[65] Com. c., Art. L 464-1.

[66] Dec. 00-MC-19, dec. 00-MC-17, dec. 00-MC-01. All decisions are available on the website and may be found through the search engine: http://www.autoritedelaconcurrence.fr/activites/avis/rechcontroles.php.

[67] Dec. 04-MC-01. See also in the telecoms sector, dec. 09-MC-02, dec. 03-MC-02, dec. 02-MC-03, dec. 01-MC- 06, dec 00-MC-19, dec. 00-MC-17, dec. 00-MC-01.

[68] Dec. 07-MC-01, 07-MC-04, 09-MC-01, 14-MC-02.

[69] Dec. 08-MC-01. The interim measures decision was followed by a commitment decision (dec. 10-D-01).

[70] Dec. 14-MC-01; see before, dec. 03-MC-01, dec. 02-MC-06.

[71] For instance in 2014, two positive decisions were adopted: the first one for broadcasting rights in sport (dec. 14-MC-01), the second one in the field of energy (dec. 14-MC-02).

[72] Requests for interim measures (2005: 14; 2006: 15; 2007: 13; 2008:21; 2009: 15; 2010: 16; 2011: 7; 2012:8; 2013:1).

23. The legal reasons can be summarized quite easily: An NCA is not the Commission... The caselaw of the Court of Justice on the lack of Community interest is fully justified at the EU level because the Commission may always rely on NCAs. A very good example was given in 2014 with the online hotel booking sector. It was clearly a case to be dealt with at the EU level,[73] but, as the Commission decided not to open its own investigation, the French, Swedish and Italian competition authorities decided to intervene instead.[74]

Furthermore, the mechanisms that deal with the allocation of cases between the Commission and NCAs, which were introduced in the Regulation 1/2003, seem to work. Good examples can be found in the two recent decisions of the General Court, the first one on Article 13, § 1,[75] the second one on Article 13, § 2.[76] An important precision was made in the second case. For the General Court, the grounds on which an NCA rejects the complaint are indifferent. Article 13, § 2, shall apply even if the complaint has not been treated by the NCA for priority reasons.

In France, due to the legality principle, Article 13 required modification of the provision relating to the rejection of complaints. Some new provisions were introduced that copy Article 13.[77] So far, these mechanisms have not been used in horizontal relations between NCAs.

24. This might be explained by the fact that the situation at the national level is quite different.

First, the generalisation of prioritisation cannot be justified by a risk of *forum shopping* between NCAs. It's true that, before the adoption of Regulation 1/2003, some commentators feared a kind of *forum shopping* within the network.[78] However, ten years later, this risk has not materialized. Anyway, a mechanism of reallocation of cases has been set up in the notice on the network,[79] and, so far, like Article 13, it has not been used in

---

[73] M. ABENHAÏM, "Most favored customer clauses and the on-line hotel booking investigation(s): The case for uniformity", *Concurrences*, No. 2015/1, pp. 14-17.

[74] ECN Brief, 1/2015.

[75] GC, 17 December 2014, T-201/11, *Si.mobil tekomunikacijske storitve*, ECLI:EU:T:2014:1096; *Europe*, 2015, comment L. IDOT, p. 77.

[76] GC, 21 January 2015, T-355/13, *easyJet Airline*, ECLI:EU:T:2015:36; *Europe*, 2015, comment L. IDOT, p. 113.

[77] Com. C., Art. L 462-8, al. 3 and 4, as modified by the Ordinance of November 2004.

[78] Among others, C.-D. EHLERMANN and I. ATANASIU (co-ed.), *7th European Competition Law Annual. Constructing the Network of EU Authorities*, Oxford, Hart Publishing, 2004.

[79] Commission Notice on cooperation within the Network of Competition Authorities, *OJEU*, 2004, No. C 101/43, sp. pts 17 and 18.

horizontal relations between NCAs, which confirms the good functioning of the system. Complainants usually knock on the right door.

Second, the situation of the complainant should be taken into consideration. If an NCA does not deal with the complaint, not for objective reasons like a mistake in the qualification of facts, but only for lack of interest, what will happen? If the case concerns another Member State, which may also be considered as a well-placed NCA, the complainant may try to make another complaint. However, in most situations, the complainant will have no other choice than suing before an ordinary court. It may be justified in some cases, mainly in vertical relations, when some provisions of an agreement are at stake, but not in all cases. Authorities and ordinary courts do not have the same means and the same powers. Private enforcement is not the equivalent of public enforcement. Furthermore, in some Member States, this choice between a Competition Authority and an ordinary court is an illusion. As I shall explain, this is one of the practical reasons which explain my new hostility to a generalised system of prioritisation.

25. Moreover, if a system of negative priorities is imposed to all NCAs, there is a serious risk of spillover effects. If there are in France a lot of quite interesting complaints, it's mainly because firms i) know that they will be examined and ii) are reluctant for many reasons to go before ordinary courts with these kinds of issues. The previous system, in which the Competition Council was viewed as a kind of specialised court, was not satisfactory. However, some corrections have been introduced and the most negative consequences have been addressed, notably the workload that was excessive compared to the Authority's human and material means.[80]

A preliminary evaluation of all complaints by a CA is very useful mainly for small and medium firms. They do not hesitate to fight big multinational firms even if they know that their complaint can be rejected. At the end, there are as many successes as failures. Without taking the examples of incumbents in markets recently open to competition, it is possible to mention the *Google* cases[81] or the *Nespresso* one.[82] By adopting commitments

---

[80] See, in all the annual reports, the preliminary remarks on the managements of cases stock.

[81] Three complaints against Google have been examined. Two were rejected (dec. 05-D-34 and, more recently, dec. 13-D-07), but one introduced by Navx was followed first by a decision of interim measures (dec. 10-MC-01), then by a commitment decision (dec. 10-D-30).

[82] Dec. 14-D-09. The press release mentions: "Following referrals from DEMB (the L'Or Espresso brand) and the Ethical Coffee Company, Nespresso has made a series of commitments lifting the barriers to entry for other coffee capsule makers – compatible with Nespresso coffee machines – as well as barriers to their growth".

decisions following complaints and sometimes requests for interim measures, the Competition Authority has prevented the foreclosure of some markets.

26. A third conclusion may be drawn. The reasons to impose a prioritisation system to all NCAs have not been well identified. No serious evaluation of pros and cons has been made. Even if the idea was accepted in principle, it would still require significant thought in order to be implemented.

B. Implementation of a prioritisation system?

27. The recommendation deals with two important issues: prioritisation criteria and the prioritisation process.

28. A consensus seems to exist on the need of *prioritisation criteria*. It mainly raises two types of issues. The first one is of course the determination of the adequate criteria. Thanks to the case law of the Court of Justice[83] and the principles published by some NCAs,[84] two main categories may be identified.

The first series covers what can be called competition criteria or criteria related to the presumed infringement. The public interest criterion is the broader one, but it may be explained and developed with other factors such as the gravity of the infringement, the effects on consumer welfare, the economic impact of the violation due to the economic sector, the structural factors of the market.[85] The repetition of a particular behaviour may also be taken into consideration.[86]

A second series of criteria are more strategic.[87] They may be internal to the authority, like the importance of creating a precedent,[88] the likelihood of finding an infringement, resource requirements.[89] They can also be

---

[83] The caselaw begins with the famous *Automec* decision (CFI, 18 September 1992, T-24/90, (1992) ECR II-2223. A synthesis of the caselaw before 2004 may be found in the notice on the handling of complaints (*op. cit.*).

[84] As previously seen (notes 29 to 33), this choice was made by the British, Irish, Dutch, Swedish, Greek Authorities.

[85] All the guidelines refer to this kind of criteria. It's developed in the Irish Principles (significance of the issue or effect of the conduct, wider economic significance of the market involved).

[86] See the Irish and the Swedish positions.

[87] See CMA Principles, B, Strategic significance; comp. Irish Principles.

[88] See the Swedish position.

[89] See CMA Principles, pts C. Risks and D. Resources; comp. the Irish position.

external, when the Authority checks whether it is well placed to deal a the case and whether alternative venues exist to take action.[90]

29. However, as the Court of Justice said in the *UFEX* case,[91] there is no exhaustive list of criteria:

"In view of the fact that the assessment of the Community interest raised by a complaint depends on the circumstances of each case, the number of criteria of assessment the Commission may refer to should not be limited, nor conversely should it be required to have recourse exclusively to certain criteria".[92]

The CMA principles are also quite clear on this topic. The list of factors to consider under different principles is illustrative and not exhaustive.[93] It's mainly a question of balance.[94]

30. Anyway, the choice of prioritisation raises a problem of transparency. Whether authorities should adopt systematic prioritisation criteria, notably by issuing notices or guiding principles, is still debated.[95] The recommendation recognises that it up to Authorities to decide.[96] This seems to be a good solution. Once again, it is a question of national culture. So far, few CAs have decided to publish general guidelines or principles.[97]

31. On the **prioritisation process** itself, the recommendation deals with two topics: the way in which complaints should be rejected (simple closure or other informal means; formal decision,[98] reasoned or not) and the judicial review that should be applied.[99]

It is clear that there is a link between both. If the case is closed by a formal decision – this is the rule for the Commission[100] – there will be a judicial review. In such cases, it is not so easy to preserve the prerogative of the Authority to set and pursue enforcement priorities. The caselaw of the Court of Justice is well known and has not significantly changed for

---

[90] See, the Swedish prioritisation guidelines, *op. cit.*, Greek notice, *op. cit.*
[91] CJEU, 4 March 1999, C-119/97 P, ECR, 1999 I-01341, ECLI:EU:C:1999:116.
[92] *Idem*, pt 79.
[93] CMA Principles, *op. cit.*, pt 2.2.
[94] *Idem.*
[95] As previously seen, this choice was made by the British, Irish, Dutch, Swedish, Greek.
[96] Recommendation, *op. cit.*, pt 5.
[97] See, note 82.
[98] The Dutch Authority only has to issue a decision when it rejects a formal complaint on the basis of the Prioritization Guidelines or on substance (see, ECN Brief, 2/2012).
[99] *Idem*, pts 3 and 4.
[100] See, the *Guérin* case, *op. cit.*

these last ten years. [101] It is not necessary to expose it again, but it may be interesting to compare it with the French so-called legality principle.

In such a system, not only is a formal decision required, but it must also be reasoned. This explains why the principle of a review before a court was never discussed. As long as the rejection is justified by objective legal reasons, the extent of the control is not in and of itself an issue. Problems arise when the referral or complaint is rejected on the basis of grounds that give rise to interpretation, like the lack of probative elements. In the nineties, the Court of Appeals of Paris was rather reluctant to reject claims for lack of sufficient proof. [102] A significant change occurred in the *Agfa* case in 2005, in which the Court of appeals endorsed the FCA's desire to reject more claims for lack of probative elements. [103] This kind of evolution cannot be decided by texts. It is the result of exchanges and discussions between authorities and judges, mainly in meetings like today.

32. It is time to conclude. Is it necessary to go further than the recommendation? My personal answer is no. Convergence of procedural rules within the ECN is of course an objective to reach. However, other issues are much more important, such as the calculation of fines and general issues of liability. These issues also include the definition of the word "undertaking" and its consequences, notably in the context of corporate reorganizations. In other words, priority setting should not be a priority.

---

[101] Among the most recent decisions, GC, 15 December 2010, *CEAHR*, T-427/08, ECR 2010 II-05865, ECLI:EU:T:2010:517; GC, 24 November 2011, *EFIM*, T-296/09, ECLI:EU:T:2011; GC, 23 November 2011, *Daphne Jones*, T-320/07, ECLI:EU:T:2011:686; GC, 9 March 2012, *Comité de défense de la viticulture charentaise*, T-192/07, ECLI:EU:T:2012:116; GC, 30 May 2013, *Omnis Group*, T-74/11, ECLI:EU:T:2013:283. The latest decisions intervened in the specific context of commitment proceedings (GC, 11 July 2013, 2 decisions, *BVGD*, joined cases, T-104/07 and T-339/08,ECLI:EU:T:2013:366, *Diamanthandel A. Spira*, joined cases, T-108/07 and T-354/08, ECLI:EU:T:2013:367; GC, 6 February 2014, *CEES*, T-342/11, ECLI:EU:T:2014:60).

[102] See, for a general study, D. BARTHE, *op. cit.*

[103] C. appeals, Paris, 17 May 2005, confirmation of dec. 04-D-60.

II

PROCEDURAL CONVERGENCE IN ANTITRUST ENFORCEMENT – IN NEED OF INCREASED COHERENCE AND EFFECTIVENESS?

PART I: TOWARDS A HIGHER STANDARD OF PROCEDURAL RIGHTS? ISSUES RELATING TO INVESTIGATIONS (LEGAL PRIVILEGE, DAWN RAIDS, REQUESTS FOR INFORMATION...)

■

Denis Waelbroeck[*]

One of the greatest achievements of Regulation 1/2003 was the harmonisation – through its Article 3 – of substantive competition law across the EU. However, so far this has not been the case for procedural rules.[1] Disparities can thus arise at every stage of the procedure, not only during the phase of decision or of detection on cases, but also during the investigation stage (*i.e.* requests for information, inspections, legal privilege, access to the file, leniency applications, etc.).[2] Clearly, this disparity raises first a number of *practical issues*, as companies acting in several jurisdictions have to confront different sets of national legal rules with all the complexity and legal uncertainty it entails. It raises also issues for the authorities in terms of effectiveness of the procedures. But finally, it may also more fundamentally lead to a number of delicate *legal problems* for the companies concerned as will be shown hereafter.

Depending on the authority in charge, the standards of protection of procedural rights will indeed widely differ, with the consequence that a decision in one Member State may be invoked in another, even if it does not meet the requirements applicable there in terms of procedural rights.

---

[*] Partner Ashurst LLP, Professor at the ULB and College of Europe in Bruges. The author expresses his gratitude to Mrs Francesca Gentile for her assistance in drafting this paper.

[1] As we have had in the past already the occasion to regret: see D. Waelbroeck, "Twelve feet all dangling down and six necks exceeding long. The EU network of competition authorities and the European Convention on Fundamental Rights", in *The EU network of Competition Authorities*, Oxford, Hart Publishing, 2005, pp. 465 *et seq.*

[2] C. Smits and D. Waelbroeck, "Le droit de la concurrence et les droits fondamentaux", in M. Soriano, *Les droit de l'homme dans les politiques de l'Union européenne*, Bruxelles, Larcier, 2006, p. 155.

As regards inspections, for instance, a national competition authority (hereafter "ANC") could ask an authority from another Member State to conduct an inspection on its behalf under a completely different set of rules than applicable in its own country in terms of inspectable premises, possibilities of tapping phone calls, judicial warrants, etc. As a result also, decisions of authorities applying diverging standards of protection can ultimately be invoked before courts of the various Member States. This raises numerous questions:

- it is not clear for instance to what extent an ANC can base itself on information that has not been collected in accordance with the standard of protection existing at its own national level;

- it is not clear either if there is any possibility for a company to object to an inspection in such circumstances – or, if not, if it has any possibility to raise the consequent illegality of any decision taken on this basis in case of litigation before the courts of other (stricter) Member States;

- nor is it clear whether an ANC can question the effectiveness of the inspections conducted on its behalf by another authority in breach of its own home-country rule or even force such other authority, on the basis of the EU principle of *"effectiveness"* to apply more effective investigation methods.

The situation is further complicated by a number of factors:

- first, as regards the binding force of a decision of one NCA before the courts of other Member States, rules applicable in some Member States are occasionally very far-reaching. This is so for instance in Germany, where decisions issued by NCAs from any Member State across the EU are considered binding under German national law.[3] At the current

---

[3]   § 33 Abs. 4 GWB: *"Wird wegen eines Verstoßes gegen eine Vorschrift dieses Gesetzes oder gegen Artikel 101 oder 102 des Vertrages über die Arbeitsweise der Europäischen Union Schadensersatz gefordert, ist das Gericht an die Feststellung des Verstoßes gebunden, wie sie in einer bestandskräftigen Entscheidung der Kartellbehörde, der Europäischen Kommission oder der Wettbewerbsbehörde oder des als solche handelnden Gerichts in einem anderen Mitgliedstaat der Europäischen Union getroffen wurde. Das Gleiche gilt für entsprechende Feststellungen in rechtskräftigen Gerichtsentscheidungen, die infolge der Anfechtung von Entscheidungen nach Satz 1 ergangen sind. Entsprechend Artikel 16 Absatz 1 Satz 4 der Verordnung (EG) Nr. 1/2003 gilt diese Verpflichtung unbeschadet der Rechte und Pflichten nach Artikel 267 des Vertrages über die Arbeitsweise der Europäischen Union"*. Initially, the draft Directive of the European Parliament and of the Council on damage actions for breach of competitive law (see eg. No. 15983/13 of 27 November 2013) provided similarly at its Article 9 that: *"1. Member States shall ensure that an infringement of competition law found by a final decision of a national competitive authority or a review court is deemed to be irrefutably established for the purpose of an action for damages brought before their national courts under Article 101 or 102 of the Treaty or under national competition law.*

stage of development of EU competition law, such a rule (which was also initially considered in the context of the draft directive on damage actions for breach of competition rules) is in our view highly questionable. In particular, it is difficult to imagine that in the absence of equal standards in all Member States, such an automatic binding effect on national courts is compliant with the over-arching requirement to respect the national fundamental rights.[4]

Given in particular that (a) a finding of infringement of Article 101 or 102 TFEU is recognised as being a finding that a "*crime*" has been committed,[5] and that (b) those findings are generally made in the first instance in most Member States by executive bodies (*i.e.* not independent courts), it is indeed quite difficult in the light of fundamental rights to make those findings binding on the courts of any Member State;

– second, the EU not being part to the ECHR, there is a further problem since its provisions cannot be invoked as a direct source of rights against EU Commission measures. This means that parties will occasionally have to deal with divergent interpretations by the Luxembourg and Strasbourg courts.[6] National courts will then be in the awkward situation that they either decide to comply with the EU Courts' case-law, with the risk that this be questioned later by the ECtHR, or decide to comply with ECHR case-law, which then may be viewed as a violation of EU law;[7]

This provision is without prejudice to the rights and obligations under Article 267 of the Treaty. 2. Member States shall ensure that a final decision referred to in paragraph 1 given in another Member State can be presented before their national court as evidence, among other, of the fact that an infringement of competitive law occurred". This proposal to make decisions of authorities binding before the court of all Member States proved to be highly controversial and in the December compromise text, the binding effect of national decision was removed. Henceforth, Member States are only obliged to accept these decisions as means of evidence in line with applicable national procedural rules.

[4] Thus, as is well-known, the German Constitutional Court for instance requires that only "*so long as*" ("*Solange*") EU law has a level of protection of fundamental rights complying substantially with the protections afforded by the German Fundamental Law, no review of Union acts in light of the German Constitution will be performed (see BVergG, *Handels-Gesellschaft*, 22 October 1986, 2 BvR 197/83). One may wonder whether the same rule should not apply *a fortiori* concerning the binding effect of a ruling by another competition authority in another Member State.

[5] See e.g. *ECtHR Menarini* judgment, 27 September 2011, Case 43509/08.

[6] See below for instance the reference to the diverging case-laws of the ECJ and the ECtHR on the privilege against self-incrimination.

[7] C. SMITS and D. WAELBROECK, "Le droit de la concurrence et les droits fondamentaux", in M. SORIANO, *Les droit de l'homme dans les politiques de l'Union européenne*, Bruxelles, Larcier, 2006, pp. 147-148.

– third, also if the Commission applies Article 11(6) of Regulation 1/2003 and initiates proceedings to relieve a NCA of its competence with the result that the parties concerned will be deprived of the protection afforded by the ECHR (including the judicial system of the ECHR), one may wonder if this is at all compatible with the ECHR.

It is true that to deal with these problems, some minimal safeguard measures have been put in place:

– first, Regulation 1/2003 expresses the principle in its Recital 37 that *"This Regulation respects the fundamental rights and observes the principles recognised in particular by the Charter of Fundamental Rights"* and that *"Accordingly, this Regulation should be interpreted and applied with respect to those rights and principles"*;

– secondly, it is expressly foreseen that information obtained through Article 12 of Regulation 1/2003 can only be used for the implementation of Articles 101 and 102 TFEU and for the purpose for which it was collected and not for instance for tax or other reasons;

– finally, pursuant to Article 12 (3) of Regulation 1/2013, information exchanged *"can only be used in evidence to impose sanctions on natural persons where the law of the transmitting authority foresees sanctions of a similar kind in relation to an infringement of [Article 101 or Article 102 TFEU] or, in the absence thereof, the information has been collected in a way which respects the same level of protection of the rights of defence of natural persons as provided for under the national rules of the receiving authority"*. Still, in this latter case, *"the information exchange cannot be used by the receiving authority to impose custodial sanctions"*. As a consequence, even in case of information obtained by means of a less restrictive national system, the information could not be used to impose a sanction on a natural person. However, in all remaining cases and in particular in case of sanctions on legal persons, this information could in principle have evidential value (although fundamental rights apply not only to natural persons, but also to legal persons).

Despite these relatively minimal safeguards and despite also the convergence encouraged by the EU Commission[8] and by ECN Reports,[9] there is

---

[8] Communication from the Commission to the European Parliament and the Council-Ten Years of Antitrust Enforcement under Regulation 1/2003: Achievements and Future Perspectives, (COM (2014) 453, 9.7.2014).

[9] A set of seven recommendations on Regulation enforcement power was endorsed within the ECN in 2013. They serve as a *"soft"* framework of reference which CAN can use see

unfortunately currently no binding instrument yet imposing a coherent and uniform system of procedural rights for the application of competition rules in Europe. True, some States have shown signs of what one could call "*spontaneous harmonization*", but these initiatives have only had a limited impact so far.

Currently, the only limit on national procedural autonomy is that Member States are obliged to respect the principles of "*effectiveness*" and "*equivalence*". As is well-known, the principle of "*effectiveness*" in particular has been used by the European Court of Justice ("ECJ"), also in the field of competition law, to impose more effective remedies. Reference can here be made for instance to the *Courage/Crehan* judgment which requires Member States to accept under certain conditions actions for damages for breach of EU competition rules.[10] *Mutatis Mutandis*, the principle of effectiveness is arguably also at the heart of what the ECJ did in the *Camera Care* case when it ruled that the Commission's power to take binding decisions in competition matters necessarily implies also the power to take interim measures.[11] Thus, on the basis of the principle of effectiveness, it could be argued that if a Member State does not give its national authorities sufficient investigatory powers (eg. not the power to seal premises or not the power to gather digital evidence), this might be illegal under EU law.

In its Staff Working Document "*Ten years of Antitrust Enforcement under Regulation 1/2003*",[12] as well as in the accompanying Communication from the Commission to the European Parliament and the Council,[13] much emphasis is put on the principle of effectiveness and on the need to enhance competition enforcement by giving NCAs stronger tools. Conversely, this Staff Working Document and this Communication make little reference to problems which procedural divergence entails for the rights of the undertakings concerned. As procedural rights are mostly fundamental rights, it is important however to keep in mind that such rights trump any consideration for greater effectiveness of procedures. The requirement of effectiveness is indeed no reason for setting aside these rights. In this

---

http://ec.europa.eu/competition/ecu/documents.html#power. The ECN endorsed recommendations on: (1) Investigative Power, Enforcement Measures and Sanctions in the context of Inspection and Request for Information; (2) the Power to Collect Digital Evidence, including by Forensic Means; (3) Assistance in Inspections conducted under Article 22(1) of Regulation (EC) No. 1/2003; (4) The Power to set Priorities; (5) Interim Measures; (6) Commitment Procedures and (7) The Power to Impose Structural Reminder.

[10] See Case C-453/99, *Courage Ltd v. Crehan*, [2001] ECLI:EU:C:2001:465.

[11] Order of 17 January 1980, *Camera Care*, [1980] ECLI:EU:C:1980:18.

[12] Doc. SWD (2014) 230/2.

[13] Doc. COM (2014) 453.

regard, it should be emphasized first that to the extent national authorities apply EU rules, they are bound to respect at the very least the guarantees recognised at EU level as a minimum standard of protection. Indeed, whenever Member States authorities act *"within the scope of application of the Treaty"*, in particular whenever measures are adopted in the field of a EU common policy such as competition, they have to do so in strict compliance with the general principles of EU law.[14] This is so *a fortiori* where Member States provide for sanctions in application of EU rules.[15] The same goes for the rights derived from the EU Charter of Fundamental Rights.

Secondly, Member States have not only to respect the general principle of EU law and the requirements of the EU Charter of Fundamental Rights but also those of the European Convention on Human Rights ("ECHR"), not only in so far as they have been taken over as general principles of EU law, but also in their capacity of signatories of the Convention.

Thirdly, to the extent the rights at stake are considered as fundamental rights in even only one single Member State, there is also a strong case to be made for accepting such rights also at EU level. Indeed, it is essential that the EU should protect the highest standard of protection of fundamental rights. Otherwise, there would indeed be a legitimate concern by Member States that the creation of the EU led to a reduction in the protection of fundamental rights in their territory (see the German *"Solange"* judgment quoted above). The ECJ therefore repeatedly stressed that it cannot accept actions which *"are incompatible with fundamental rights recognised and protected by the Constitution of the Member States"*.[16] Thus, if any Member State considers a principle to be of such importance as to be a *"fundamental right"* or to incorporate it in its own Constitution, it should clearly be accepted as a general principle of EU law. As just indicated, this will precisely be the case for many procedural rights of parties in inspections by competition authorities.

Finally, from a more general perspective, emphasis cannot be put enough on the importance of the rule of law and of adequate procedures to achieve

---

[14]   See eg. Case C-2/92, *The Queen v. Ministry of Agriculture, Fisheries and Food, ex parte Dennis Clifford Bostock* [1994] ECLI:EU:C:1994:116, § 16; Case C-5/88, *Wachauf v. Bundesamt für Ernährung und Forstwirtschaft* [1989] ECLI:EU:C:1989:18, § 19; Case C-351/92, *Graff v. Hauptzollamt Köln Rheinau* [1994] ECLI:EU:C:1994:293, § 17; Case C-292/97, *Karlsson and Others* [2000] ECLI:EU:C:2000:202. §§ 35-37; see in more detail H. SCHERMERS and D. WAELBROECK, *Judicial Protection in the EU*, 6th ed. 2001, Waterloo, Kluwer, §§ 70-71. See also Commission Notice on the cooperation between the Commission and the Courts of the EU Member States in the application of [Articles 101 and 102 TFEU], *OJ* No. C101, 2004, § 35.

[15]   Case C-29/95, *Pastoors and Trans-Cap v. Belgische Staat*, [1997] ECLI:EU:C:1997:28, § 24.

[16]   Case C-4/73, *Nold KG v. Commission*, [1982] ECLI:EU:C:1974:51.

good law. In a network of 29 authorities, applying moreover a law that is as uncertain and prone to political interference as competition law can be, good procedures are critical to obtain coherent and predictable decisions in a convergent manner throughout the European Union. Harmonising procedures to achieve adequate protection for the parties concerned is therefore critical for the sound operation of the network.

The above sets the scene for some of the difficulties that may arise where 29 authorities are supposed to apply the same law under different procedural rules.

In so far as the present paper is devoted to the problem of investigations in particular, we have chosen to focus hereafter on some more topical queries in particular, *i.e.* the issue of Legal Professional Privilege ("LPP") (I), the issue of inspections (II), and the issue of requests for information (III).

I. The legal Professional Privilege ("LPP")

Currently, there is no statutory provision in the EU establishing LPP across the 28 Member States. Although the latter was recognized in reliance on Articles 6 and 8 of the ECHR as a fundamental right by the ECJ some thirty years ago in *AM&S v. European Commission*[17] there has also been surprisingly little case law since on LPP at European level. Moreover, whilst it is true that, in nearly all jurisdictions,[18] NCA's respect in theory LPP,[19] those rights are subject to very different conditions in practice depending on the Member State concerned.

As will be discussed hereafter, the main elements of divergence relate to the scope of application of LPP (A). We will then examine what impact this has on disclosure of documents between competition authorities (B) and before national courts (C).

A. Scope of application

As regards the scope of application of LPP, there are in particular three elements that should be taken into consideration, *i.e.* (1) the definition of

---

[17] Case C-155/79, *AM & S Europe Limited v. Commission of the European Communities*, [1974] ECLI:EU:C:1982:157.

[18] J. Holtz, "Legal Professional Privilege in Europe: a Missed Policy Opportunity", *Journal of European Competition Law & Practice*, 2013, p. 4.

[19] See ECN Investigative Power Report, 31 October 2012, §§ 2-5.

"*lawyer*", (2) the notion of "*client*", and (3) the precise definition of the documents to which LPP applies. With regard to the three, differences are sometimes significant between European and national regimes.

1. Definition of "lawyer"

At EU level, LPP does not extend under current case-law to "*in-house*" lawyers,[20] nor to non- EU lawyers.[21] At national level however, situations differ. Thus, some countries are recognising LPP to "*in-house*" lawyers; some countries are also recognising LPP to non-EU lawyers.

(i) "In-house" lawyers

In a number of jurisdictions (for instance in UK, Ireland, Portugal, etc.),[22] "*in-house*" lawyer's documents are privileged. This protection is regarded by them as a fundamental right both under Article 6 and Article 8 ECHR. The restrictive interpretation given by the ECJ is in fact not shared by an increasing number of national courts. Interestingly, the need to recognise LPP to in-house lawyers has for instance recently been confirmed force-fully by two decisions by respectively the Brussels Court of Appeal and the Dutch Supreme Court (as discussed hereafter). There are also interesting developments of the German case-law in this regard which we will mention.

In the Belgian *Belgacom case*,[23] the Brussels Court of Appeal thus recognized LPP to "*in-house*" lawyers subject to certain conditions.[24] The Court of Appeal dismissed the application of the restrictive ECJ case law to the Belgian competition authority, including when this procedure is being conducted in order to establish an infringement of EU competition law. According to the Court of Appeal, the existence of separate legal orders (the national one and the EU legal one) is a sufficient reason for applying different rules between the two concerning the protection of advice by "*in-house*" lawyers.

---

[20] Joined cases T-125/03 and T-253/03, *Akzo Nobel Chemicals Ltd and Akcros Chemicals v. Commission of the European Communities*, [2007] ECLI:EU:T:2007:287 and on appeal, Case C-550/07 P, [2010] ECLI:EU:C:2010:512.

[21] *See* note 16. After the creation of the EEA in 1994, the privilege was extended to EEA-lawyers.

[22] See ECN Investigative Powers Report, 31 October 2012, § 2.5.

[23] Brussels Court of Appeal, 18th Chamber, Case 2011/MR/3-*Belgacom*, 5 March 2013.

[24] *See* S. STRIEVI and C. SMITS, "État des lieux en matière de perquisition après l'arrêt *Belgacom* du 5 mars 2013", *TBM/RCB* 2013/4, p. 379.

In this case, the Court of Appeal recognised the privilege attached to communications between a lawyer and his client as a fundamental right ensured by Article 8 ECHR and Article 7 of the EU Charter of Fundamental Rights. Such communications may not therefore be seized by the Belgian competition authority during a search, regardless of whether the inquiry aims at establishing an infringement of national law or of European law.

On the contrary, and as a result of the ECJ case-law (in *AM&S, Akzo, etc.*), EU officials – whether acting alone or assisted by agents of a national competition authority – are not obliged to respect the LPP granted by Belgian law to *"in-house"* lawyers, even when they are conducting a raid in Belgium. However, in the event of the Belgian competition authority conducting a search at the request of the Commission, Article 22 of Regulation 1/2003[25] indicates that investigators *"shall exercise their power in accordance with their national law"*. This is so even when they are conducting inspections on behalf of another NCA or of the Commission. The Brussels Court of Appeal finds in this provision the confirmation that national law and EU legislation relating to inspections – and thus the confidentiality of the seized documents – may differ depending on the authority conducting the raid.

In the Netherlands, the Supreme Court similarly ruled in the *Delta* case[26] that an *"in-house"* lawyer in the Netherlands benefits from the LPP if regularly registered as an attorney with the Dutch Bar. The Supreme Court primarily reached its conclusion on the basis of the professional rules that apply to in-house lawyers, notably focusing on the principle of independence. However, it is still unclear whether such a privilege can apply to in-house lawyers who work in the Netherlands, but are registered with a bar association based outside this jurisdiction.

Finally with regard to Germany, as in the *Akzo* judgment, German courts have generally pointed to the lack of independence of *"in-house"* lawyers to deny them LPP protection. However, recently, the Regional Court in Bonn[27] established that LPP may be extended to *"in-house"* lawyers when there is evidence of a special relationship with the client, wherein the client has given actual instructions for a specific case, and is not just an *"in-house"* attorney dealing with wide-ranging work for the client concerned. This is

---

[25] Council Regulation (EC) No. 1/2003 of 16 December 2002 on the implementation of the rules on competition laid down in Articles [101] and [102] of the Treaty, available at: http://eur-lex.europa.eu/LexUriServ/LexUriServ.do?uri=OJ:l:2003:001:0001:0025:en:PDF.

[26] Case *Delta v. Stichting H9 Invest*, ECLI:NL:PHR:2013:BY6101.

[27] Regional Court of Bonn, Decision of 29 September 2005, 37 Qs 27/05; see also *LG Berlin*, WISTRA 2006, 158, §§ 15-16.

designed to ensure that the *"in-house"* lawyer has sufficient independence to be able to give legal advice on a very specific situation. It remains however to be seen whether other courts in Germany will follow suit.

Arguably, as a result of these different national developments, one can wonder whether there could not possibly one day be an emerging *"common tradition"* as considered necessary by the Court of to widen the principles set out in *Akzo*.[28]

(ii) Non-EU (EEA) lawyers

As indicated, the EU LPP (under the *AM&S case* law) extends only to communications with EU (EEA)-qualified lawyers and not to those with non-EU (EEA) lawyers.

A similar principle has been recently applied by the Swiss Supreme Court who has excluded the benefit of LPP to a non-Swiss lawyer (the LPP however is extended under Swiss Law – and in particular under Articles 4 and 21 FAFML – to EU/EFTA lawyers, but not to lawyers from other jurisdictions).[29]

However, in some Member States such limitation to EU/EEA lawyers does not apply.

In the UK, for instance, the protection covers communication with any lawyer regardless of the bar (or the law society) to which he belongs. British courts will in fact, only ascertain the privilege status of a document under UK law and not in the reference to EU law (it does not matter whether LPP may have been claimed and/or accepted before a foreign court, provided that the confidentiality of the document has been maintained since its creation and that it has not been disclosed).

They will not enforce a foreign disclosure order in relation to privileged documents located in the UK, if it goes against UK law. The problem is of course that a privileged document under UK law may become disclosable before a foreign court depending on the national rules applied by that court.[30]

---

[28] *See* note 16, the judgment of the ECJ at para. 69 referring to the need to *"take into account the principles and concepts common to the laws of the Member States concerning observance of confidentiality"*.

[29] Swiss Federal Supreme Court, ATF 140 II 102, 6 December 2013.

[30] C. JAN, "Legal privilege: what it means in the UK, UK/US and UK/EU", 25th January 2013, available at: http://www.kingsleynapley.co.uk/news-and-events/blogs/dispute-resolution-law-blog/legal-privilege-what-it-means-in-the-uk-uk-us-and-uk-eu.

2. Notion of "client"

Although the question of which person can be regarded as a *"client"* whose correspondence with a lawyer is protected, has not yet been examined at by European courts, it should be noted that this notion of client is interpreted differently in some Member States.

For instance, in the UK, following the *"Three Rivers"* House of Lords decision,[31] the notion of client has been restricted to a limited group of persons which are part of the organisation the lawyer is acting for (for instance, only senior employees and not any member of the organization).

3. Documents to which LPP applies

According to the European Court of Human Rights ("ECtHR"), any correspondence between a lawyer and his client is protected, whatever the nature of the exchange.[32] There have been numerous judgments of the ECtHR concerning inspections at a lawyer's office,[33] interception of the correspondence between a lawyer and his client,[34] tapping of a lawyer's phone calls,[35] the search and securing of electronic documents in a lawyer's office,[36] etc.

Similarly, at EU level, the nature of the documents to which LPP applies has been clarified to some extent in the *Hilti*[37] and *Akzo*[38] judgements. Thus, in *Hilti* for instance, the ECJ stated that any internal document reporting the content of advice from outside counsel qualifying for the legal privilege also benefits from the same protection. Also, in accordance with the *Akzo* judgment, documents preparatory to requests for legal advice are protected.

However, the nature of documents that are protected has received sometimes broadly diverging interpretations at national level, between a very restrictive conception for instance by the German authorities to a broader approach applied in other Member States such as the UK.

---

[31] *Three Rivers District Council v. The Governor & Company of The Bank of England* (No. 5) [2003] EWCA Civ 474.

[32] ECtHR, *Michaud*, judgment of 6 December 2012, §§ 117-119.

[33] ECtHR, *Niemitz*, judgment of 16 December 1992.

[34] ECtHR, *Schönenberger and Durmaz*, judgment of 20 June 1998.

[35] ECtHR, *Kopp*, judgment of 25 March 1998.

[36] ECtHR, *Sallinen*, 27 September 2005.

[37] In Case T-30/89, *Hilti v. Commission*, [1990] ECLI:EU:C:1991:70.

[38] In Joined cases T-125/03 and T-253/03, *Akzo Nobel Chemicals Ltd and Akcros Chemicals Ltd v. Commission*, the ECJ affirmed that documents issued by the client to allow the lawyer to prepare his advice, are protected as long as the undertaking is able to prove their direct link to its defense.

In Germany, courts grant LPP only under rather strict conditions.[39] German courts found that both under the German Code of Criminal Procedure ("CCP"), under the German Constitution and under Article 6(3) ECHR, the LPP right protects only documents that have been produced by outside lawyers after the initiation of competition proceedings and in their context. This excludes, for instance, internal audit documents or investigations.[40]

As to *the UK* legal order, it is indeed interesting to note that it is much broader and distinguishes between two very different kinds of privilege: the *"legal advice privilege"* and the *"litigation privilege"*. The former covers communications between a solicitor and his client pertaining to the giving or receiving of legal advice, whilst the second is wider and applies to any document created to prepare the defence once litigation has started. Litigation privilege applies not merely to communications between a solicitor and his client but extends to communications with third parties such as expert witnesses.[41] This second privilege has been recognized so as to ensure a fair trial within the adversarial system of justice.[42]

No similar difference has however yet been recognised at the EU level.

B. Disclosure of documents between competition authorities

The above mentioned differences in the recognition of LLP across the EU raise a number of problems as regards relationships within the ECN.

Thus, under Article 12(1) of Regulation 1/2003, the competition authorities of the ECN have the power to exchange and use information collected for the purpose of applying competition law. For the purpose of applying Articles 101 and 102 TFEU, the Commission and the competition authorities of the Member States shall in other words have the power to provide one another with and use in evidence factual information, including of a confidential nature.

---

[39] C. Swaak, *"Legal Privilege: An Overview of EU and national case law"*, e-Competitions, No. 65144, available at: http://www.concurrences.com.

[40] Regional Court Bonn, Decision of 12 June 2012, 27 Qs 2/12. *See* I. Oest and A. German, "Regional Court refuses to extend the protection of legal privilege to internal audit documents", 12 June 2012, *e-Competitions Bulletin*, June 2012, Art. No. 49699.

[41] For instance in the *OFT v. Tesco* case: interviews given after the opening of the proceeding (CAT 6, *Tesco Stores Ltd, Tesco Holdings Ltd, & Tesco Plc v. Office of Fair Trading* [2012], Case No. 1188/1/1/11).

[42] V. Annetta and N. Ryan-Green, "Privilege limited in commission of inquiry", 2nd August 2006, available at: http://www.claytonutz.com/publications/newsletters/litigation_and_dispute_resolution_insights/20060802/privilege_limited_in_commission_of_inquiry.page.

NCAs may even use information exchanged within the ECN in order to enforce their national competition law when it is applied in parallel with EU law and does not lead to a different outcome.

Such a procedure has implications on the treatment of LPP. An NCA is indeed able to obtain and in theory even possibly use a document obtained from an authority in another Member State which is subject to less strict LPP rules than those it is bound itself to apply. True, an obligation of professional secrecy is in practice foreseen in all Member States as well as at EU level,[43] and moreover it is accepted that the term *"professional* secrecy" used in Article 28 of Regulation 1/2003 is an *"EU law concept"* and includes in particular business secrets and other confidential information so that *"this will create a common minimum level of protection throughout the European Commission"*;[44] still the EU concept is less protective than that applicable in some Member States.

This means that, apart from the above-mentioned narrow exceptions in Article 12 (3) of Regulation 1/2003 (*i.e.* (a) that if *"sanctions on natural persons"* are imposed, the transmitting authority may use the document only if it has similar sanctions for such infringement in its own legal system, or (b) alternatively if the rights applicable in the Member States receiving the information are the same), there is a risk that the scope of LPP in the EU could in theory to some extent be circumvented via exchanges of information within the ECN.

C. Disclosure of documents before national courts

A probably even more worrying aspect to consider in future is the disclosure of documents to third parties before national courts in the context of private damages claims.

In this regard, the current push for private enforcement of competition law within the EU exposes undertakings more than ever to the possibility of their documents being obtained by third parties and being used against them in civil damages claims for competition law infringements.[45]

---

[43] See Commission Notice on cooperation within the ECN, at § 28(a).

[44] Commission Notice on Cooperation within the Network of Competition Authorities, (2004/C 101/03), § 28.

[45] The Legal Privilege Handbook 2013, p. 6-7, available at: http://www.dlapiper.com/~/media/Files/Insights/Publications/2013/04/Legal%20Privilege%20Handbook%202013/Files/DLA_Piper_Legal_Privilege_Handbook_2013/FileAttachment/DLA_Piper_Legal_Privilege_Handbook_2013.pdf.

In fact, correspondence with lawyers may be caught by the far-reaching rules of the Directive on Antitrust Damage Actions[46] relating to mandatory disclosure of evidence (Articles 5 to 8). This is so all the more as the Directive does not create a clear system for the protection of the documents at stake. True, Article 5(5) provides that *"Member States shall ensure that national courts give ful effect to applicable legal professional privilege under Union or national law when ordering the disclosure of evidence"*. However, LPP is not defined in the Directive. Moreover, Article 5(8) provides that *"this Article shall not prevent Member States from maintaining or introducing rules which would lead to wide disclosure of evidence"*. As a result, there is a significant risk that documents protected under LPP in one Member State might be improperly used in the context of a damage litigation and even in other contexts later.

In *Donau-Chemie*,[47] the ECJ found in addition that any *per se* protection of documents would be incompatible with primary law as it could violate the principle of effectiveness regarding the right to compensation: *"in exercising their powers for the purpose of applying national rules on the right of access, by persons believing themselves to be adversely affected by a cartel, to documents relating to national proceedings concerning that cartel, the national courts must weigh up the respective interests in favour of disclosure of the information and in favour of the protection of that information (see, to that effect, Pfeiderer, paragraph 30). That weighing-up is necessary because, in competition law in particular, any rule that is rigid, either by providing for absolute refusal to grant access to the documents in question or for granting access to those documents as matter of course, is liable to undermine the effective application of, inter alia, Article 101 TFEU and the rights that provision confers on individuals"*.

The fact that the Directive does not harmonise the divergent Member State regime on LPP might thus in practice have a considerable impact on applicable national rules. For instance, as regards the litigation privilege existing in the UK, the right to consider any defensive document created after the beginning of the litigation as privileged, might not necessarily be easy to guarantee in light of the less protective EU rules on LPP.

---

[46] Directive of the European Parliament and of the Council on certain rules governing actions for damages under national law for infringements of the competition law provisions of the Member States and of the European Union, 2013/0185 (COD). PE-CONS 80/14. FC/vm DGG 3B RC 8. JUSTCIV 80. CODEC 961.

[47] Case C-536/11, *Bundeswettbewerbsbehörde v. Donau Chemie AG and Others*, [2013] ECLI:EU:C:2013:366, at §§ 30-31.

True, the European Commission and the ECJ have in general taken a restrictive view on accessible documents in competition cases. Thus, they have restricted access to the European Commission's files in competition proceedings by applying extensively the exceptions foreseen in the Transparency Regulation 1049/2001 related to the scope of particular acts (e.g. undermining the protection of public interest or the protection of commercial interests of a natural or legal person or the institution's decision making-process). In other words, case-law has shown a certain prevalence of EU competition law requirements over the Transparency Regulation regarding public access to documents.

For instance, in case T-380/08, *The Netherlands v. Commission*,[48] access to the non-confidential version of the EU Commission decision to the Dutch government was denied. The General Court considered that, as long as a cartel decision is subject to judicial review, an undertaking has a right to keep it confidential. Since a request for access to documents under the Transparency Regulation, the purpose of which is to enable the requesting party to seek damages for cartel violation, pursues a private interest, the Court found that it does not fulfil the overriding public interest criteria.

Still, the General Court considered that access to cartel documents should be arbitrated by the national court before which an action for damages has been lodged.[49] In accordance with Article 15 of Regulation 1/2003, national courts may in doing so ask the EU Commission to transmit to them relevant information in its possession.

Whilst the General Court has thus been restrictive before allowing for an expanded access to EU Commission cartel documents under the Transparency Regulation,[50] there remain a number of uncertainties. Thus, if a plaintiff wants access to documents relevant to its (potential) case, it must seek them under the national rules of civil procedure.[51] In so doing, and in the absence of EU-wide legislation on the question, national courts have to decide on a case-by-case basis and in accordance with their national procedural laws, the level of access a civil plaintiff should have to documents submitted under a cartel leniency program.

---

[48] Case T-380/08, *Kingdom of the Netherlands v. Commission*, [2013] ECLI:EU:T:2013:480.
[49] See *Pfleiderer* case quoted above.
[50] Y. Botteman, "A Need to Know Basis: The European Commission's Approach to Sharing Information Concerning Article 101 TFEU Infringements", 4 October 2013, available at: http://www.steptoe.com/publications-9074.html.
[51] As foreseen in the Case C-360/09, *Pfleiderer AG v. Commission*, [2011] ECLI:EU:C:2011:389.

Beyond the issue of LPP, there are however many other problems under the current system of national procedural autonomy. Another example discussed hereafter thus concerns inspections:

II. Inspections

As is well-known, Regulation 1/2003 has increased to some extent the investigatory powers of the EU Commission, in particular by allowing inspections of private premises, affixing of seals and conducting interviews. These powers are not all granted to all NCAs at national level. In its Staff working Document *"Enhancing competition enforcement by the Member States' competition authorities"*,[52] emphasis is put by the Commission on the fact that NCAs should have all necessary powers replicating those of the Commission, e.g. *"some NCAs cannot inspect non-business premises, [...], some NCAs do not have the power to seal premises, to effectively gather digital evidence and/or to inspect non-suspected undertakings [...], they are unable to enforce their power to impact, e.g. they cannot request assistance of the police if an undertaking refuses to submit to an inspection"*.

The Commission stresses in particular that *"some authorities cannot gather digital data stored on mobile phone or cannot take forensic images or face other limitations depending on where and how data is stored, e.g. when information is accessible for the undertaking from the inspected premises, but the storage media is claimed to be physically located outside the territory of the authority"*. Thus, there are clearly in the Commission's mind issues as regards the NCAs' powers to conduct effective inspections. The Commission as a result argues for more extensive powers given to NCAs.[53]

From the companies' perspective, there are however other issues concerning the protection of their own fundamental rights of which we will highlight two hereafter, *i.e.*:

- the need for a search warrant; and
- the prohibition of *"fishing expeditions"*.

Indeed, whilst the Commission acknowledges that its fining decisions are of a criminal nature under the ECHR, the question is whether these

---

[52] Doc. SWD (2014) 231/2.
[53] See above quoted Communication from the European Commission to the European Parliament and the Council, Doc. COM (2014) 453.

decisions, as well as the procedure leading to their adoption, are in compliance with the standards mandated under the ECHR.

A. The need for a search warrant

So far, under EU law, the existence of a search warrant is not a precondition for a dawn-raid. Under Article 20 (6) of Regulation 1/2003, when the inspectors find that an undertaking opposes an inspection ordered by the Commission, *"the Member State concerned shall afford them the necessary assistance, requesting where appropriate the assistance of the police or of an equivalent enforcement authority, so as to enable them to conduct their inspection"*. It is only if such assistance is requested that a judicial warrant may be required if this is mandatory under the law of the Member State concerned (see Article 20 (7) of Regulation 1/2003). As a matter of fact, it follows that a company objecting to an inspection without prior authorization of the national court, may be exposed to a procedure to sanction its obstruction of the investigation, as was the case for instance for company *Sanofi Aventis* in 2008.[54]

However, it is unclear that these EU rules (or indeed those applicable in Member States) are at all compliant with Article 8 ECHR.

Thus, it is interesting to note that the ECtHR has very recently ruled on the necessity of a prior search warrant in antitrust investigations in case *Delta Pekárny A.S. v. Czech Republic.*[55]

In this case, the ECtHR condemned the Czech Republic for breach of Article 8 ECHR linked to the lack of a prior authorization for an inspection and of a sufficient *ex post* judicial review. Thus, the ECtHR ruled that dawn-raids carried out in a Czech antitrust probe in 2003 infringed the fundamental right to privacy.

The Court considered that absent an *ex ante* authorization of a judge, or alternatively of an effective review *ex post* of the necessity of the contested measure (and in case of a finding that the measure was inappropriate of a ruling providing for destruction of the copies obtained), these procedural guarantees were not sufficient to prevent the risk of an abuse of power on the part of the competition authority.

---

[54] European Commission, "Antitrust: Commission opens formal proceedings against sanofi-aventis for possible procedural infringement", MEMO/08/357, 2nd June 2008.
[55] ECtHR, 2nd October 2014, *Delta Pekárny A.S. v. République Tchèque*, No. 97/11.

On the basis of these elements, the ECtHR concluded that the *ex post* judicial review did not offer the applicant company sufficient guarantees against arbitrariness, such that the interference in its rights could be considered as proportionate to the legitimate aim pursued.

True, it follows from this case-law that the absence of a mandate can be balanced by a subsequent efficient control on the legality and the necessity of this measure. In this regard, the question will however be whether the ECJ's control over the EU Commission's decisions – as currently conducted – is sufficient, and whether in particular an inspection is justified by the facts that led the authority to conduct the inspection.[56]

The question will also be whether the exercise by the NCA of its power to assess the scope of the inspection is subject to sufficient judicial review. As such, in the *Delta Pekárny* case, the finding of the Czech district court that the inspection was justified for the reason that the authority had *"suspicions"* that a given conduct on the market was the result of a *"contact"* between competitors and that the existence or not of such a contact could only be demonstrated by evidence obtained during the inspection. This was not considered sufficient by the ECtHR.

Clearly, this case-law might have an important impact on the investigative powers of the Commission as well as a significant number of NCAs and represents an important step forward with respect to the case-law on the issue.

In *Deutsche Bahn*,[57] for instance, the EU General Court rejected the request to invalidate three inspections by the European Commission at the premises of a company and its subsidiaries. The basis of these inspections was based on the provisions of Article 20 (4) of Regulation 1/2003 that does not provide for prior judicial authorization.[58] The EU General Court held that the lack of such a prior judicial permission will not normally result in the unlawfulness of an inspection and pointed out that the absence of prior judicial authorisation is counterbalanced by *"adequate guarantees"* which constitute a sufficiently strict framework for the Commission's

---

[56] See *mutatis mutandis* ECtHR, *Société Canal Plus et autres c. France*, No. 29408/08, at § 36. In this case, the Court recognized the margin of appreciation of the Authority to conduct inspections based on facts and documents sustaining the presumption of anticompetitive practices.
[57] Joined cases T-289/11, T-290/11 and T-521/11, *Deutsche Bahn and Others v. Commission*, [2013] ECLI:EU:T:2013:404.
[58] Contrary to paragraphs 6-8 of the same Article applicable after opposition to the inspection, or to Article 21, which requires a warrant so that the national judge will then make a review of the proportionality of the coercive measures envisaged.

investigation powers and referred to (a) the statement of reasons for order-ing the inspection; (b) the need for the Commission to respect certain limits while carrying out an investigation; (c) the inability to carry out investigations by force; (d) the additional control at national level; (e) and the *ex post* judicial review.

B. The prohibition of *"fishing expeditions"*

It is well established that a decision ordering an inspection must be drafted carefully. The main characteristics of the matter being investigated must be set out so as to allow the undertaking concerned to understand its scope and to safeguard its rights of defence. It is essential indeed that the investigator must restrict his researches to the activities concerned. Language that is too broad or imprecise will not be admissible. Otherwise EU Courts may annul the decision.[59]

As recently stressed by the EU General Court in *Cementos Portland*[60] *"[...] l'existence d'une protection contre des interventions de la puis-sance publique dans la sphère d'activité privée d'une personne, qu'elle soit physique ou morale, qui seraient arbitraires ou disproportionnées constitue un principe général du droit de l'Union (arrêt du Tribunal du 22 mars 2012, Slovak Telekom/Commission, T 458/09 et T 171/10, non encore publié au Recueil, point 81). [...] Or, aux fins de respecter ce principe général,* une décision de demande de renseignements doit viser à recueillir la documentation nécessaire pour vérifier la réalité et la portée de situations de fait et de droit déterminées à propos desquelles la Commission dispose déjà d'informations, constituant des indices suf-fisamment sérieux permettant de suspecter une infraction aux règles de concurrence *(voir en ce sens et par analogie arrêt de la Cour du 22 octo-bre 2002, Roquette Frères, C 94/00, Rec., p. I-9011, points 54 et 55)".*

The General Court insisted in that judgment (§ 43) on the fact that the Commission should have sufficient indications giving raise to a *"reason-able suspicion"* of an infringment. Similarly in *Nexans*,[61] the General Court made the point that: *"(...) if the Commission were not subject to that restriction, it would in practice be able, every time it has indicia*

---

[59] Case T-135/09, *Nexans France SAS and Nexans SA v. European Commission*, [2012] ECLI:EU:T:2012:596 and Case T-140/09, *Prysmian SpA and Prysmian Cavi e Sistemi Energia Srl v. European Commission*, [2012] ECLI:EU:T:2012:597.

[60] Case T-296/11, *Cementos Portland Valderrivas, SA v. European Commission*, [2014] ECLI:EU:T:2014:121, §§ 39-40.

[61] Quoted above, at §§ 65-67.

suggesting that an undertaking has infringed the competition rules in a specific field of its activities, to carry out an inspection covering all those activities, with the ultimate aim of detecting any infringement of those rules which might have been committed by that undertaking. That is incompatible with the protection of the sphere or private activity of legal persons, guaranteed as a fundamental right in a democratic society. [...] It must therefore be held that, in the present case, the Commission was under an obligation, in order to adopt the inspection decision, to have reasonable grounds to justify an inspection at the applicants' premises [...]". The same idea was expressed by the Commission in its Green book on the presumption of innocence.[62]

Similar prohibitions of *"fishing expeditions"* exist at national level, but – again – may be more or less strict depending on the Member State concerned. In its *Belgacom* judgment[63] for instance, the Brussels Court of Appeal was quite demanding and found that the relevant decision ordering the inspection was *"manifestly too broad"*. It led indeed to the copy by the authority of some 760.000 e-mails and other digital documents, which – even if only read superficially – would require tens of thousands of working hours. The Court of Appeal found accordingly that the key-words used were too broad and did not comply with the requirements of precision, adequateness and proportionality.

Similarly in the Netherlands, the Hague District Court found that the Dutch Competition Authority was not entitled to order a forensic IT firm to produce a list of all companies in a given sector for which it had conducted compliance audits.[64] Since no reasonable suspicion of cartel participation had been put forward, the measure was held to be a pure *"fishing expedition"* prohibited by law.

Still in the same vein, in the *K**** and *B**** cases, the Austrian Supreme Court found equally recently that three newspaper articles, information called from an Internet forum and a retailer's website was not sufficient to create a *"suspicion"* justifying raiding companies in the bicycle industry.[65]

Finally, in the above General *Delta Pezárny* case, the ECtHR similarly found that a dawnraid conducted by the Czech Competition authority was

---

[62] Document of 26 April 2006, COM (2006) 174 final, § 2.6.
[63] Court of Appeal, Brussels, judgment of 5 March 2013, *Belgacom*.
[64] See President of The Hague District Court in interim injunction proceedings, ECLI:NL:RBSGR:2012:BX9781.
[65] Judgement of 6 May 2014, ECLI:AT:OGH0002:2014:RS0129421.

too broad and infringed the company's right to a fair trial as well as the employee's right to a private life.

These various decisions should clearly show the way as to the demanding conditions applicable before an inspection is ordered. They also indicate that there may be a need to define at EU level a clearer and possibly stricter framework that respects the requirements existing at national level.

III. Requests for information

Requests for information raise similarly a number of questions.

At EU level, the privilege against self-incrimination (*nemo tenetur*) has been recognised in a number of ECJ judgments.[66] According to the *Orkem* case-law,[67] "*the Commission may not compel an undertaking to provide it with answers which might involve an admission on its part of the existence of an infringement which it is incumbent upon the Commission to prove*" (§ 35). However, the ECJ also found that the Commission is entitled "*to compel an undertaking to provide all necessary information concerning such facto as may be known to it and to disclose to it, if necessary, such documents relating thereto as are in its possession, even if the latter may be used to establish, against it or another undertaking the existence of anti-competitive conduct*" (§ 34). This judgment and following case-law serve to illustrate the significant differences between the jurisprudence of the EU Court and that of the ECtHR on this question. Thus, the (then) EC Court of First Instance considered that "*the mere fact of being obliged to answer purely factual questions put by the Commission and to comply with its requests for the production of documents already in existence cannot constitute a breach of the principle of respect for the rights of defence or impair the right to a fair legal process, which offer, in the specific field of competition law, protection equivalent to that guaranteed by Article 6 of the Convention. There is nothing to prevent the addressee of a request for information from showing, whether later during the administrative procedure as in proceedings before the Community Courts, when exercising his right of defence, that the facts set out in his replies or the documents produced by him have a different meaning from that ascribed to them by the Commission (Mannesmannröhren Werke v. Commission [...],*

---

[66] See e.g. Case C-301/04 P, *Commission v. SGL*, [2006] ECLI:EU:C:2006:432.
[67] Case C-374/87, *Orkem v. Commission*, [1989] ECLI:EU:C:1989:387.

paragraphs 77 and 78)".[68] There is thus a contradiction between the position of the EU Courts which do not recognise an absolute *"right to silence"* and that of the ECtHR.[69] According to the latter, this right concerns also *"factual questions"* whilst the EU Courts recognise the duty of undertakings to provide documents and factual information to the Commission under Article 18(3) of Regulation 1/2003 even where they are incriminating.

The difference becomes even wider when reference is made to the systems applicable in the 28 Member States. In this regard, whilst the privilege against self-incrimination is protected in the majority of Member States,[70] it appears that in practice – as shown by the ECN Investigative Powers Report – the degree of protection varies widely.[71]

IV. Conclusion

As illustrated in this paper, the boundaries of investigation powers in competition cases are evolving. The main driving force in this regard flows from judicial decisions of both Member States and the ECtHR. However, in spite of these decisions, it is clear that the debate has just begun and many questions remain still open.

In fact, as pointed out above, procedural rights are not equally protected in all Member States with the consequence that, for instance, a document covered by LPP according to the restrictive case-law of the ECJ, will not necessarily be recognized as such in all Member States. Conversely, some Member States have a wide recognition of LPP than the ECJ. The concern is that these LPP rules in national legislation might in practice be circumvented through the exchange of information within the ECN or through national court decisions.

In a framework where there are no binding rules for assigning cases among authorities and where procedural guarantees are often of a variable content, multiple issues under fundamental rights may arise. This is so in particular in an institutional system conferring to the European Commission

---

[68] Joined cases T-236/01, T-239/01, T-244/01 to T-246/01, T-251/01 and T-252/01, *Tokai Carbon Co. Ltd and others v. Commission*, [2004] ECLI:EU:T:2004:118.

[69] See ECtHR, *Funke*, 25 February 1993, Series A/256-A; *Murray*, 8 February 1996, *Rec.*, 1996-I; *Saunders*, 17 December 1996, *Rec.*, 1996-VI; *Servès*, 20 October 1997, *Rec.*, 1997-VI.

[70] See ECN Investigative Powers Report, 31 October 2012, § 4.2.2.

[71] See already the Opinion of Advocate General Darmon of 18 May 1989 in the above quoted *Orkem* case, at §§ 48 to 117. See more recently the ECN Investigative Powers Report, 31 October 2012, § 4.2.2 and § 5.4.

and to a number of NCAs double duty as judge and prosecutor, where there is an increased need for a particularly extensive control of their decisions by the courts. In such a framework it is clear that the uniform interpretation and application of LPP in the EU would be beneficial.

As regards search warrants, recent decisions by the ECtHR are paving a way to a new interpretation of competition authorities with regard to the conduct of inspections. The focus is set on parties' rights and on the need of sufficient *ex post* judicial control.

The same goes for the prohibition of *"fishing expeditions"* or for the prohibition of self-incriminatory questions.

All these considerations speak for the necessity of further clarifications on these issues. As already stated, good procedures are the best guarantee for good law. And if the ECN is certainly a great achievement, practice shows that decisions are often diverging among authorities. It is our belief that better procedural guarantees would be a key element in ensuring more consistent decision making throughout the ECN. Although we recognise that proper procedures may sometimes be perceived as burdensome, quality should prevail over quantity. After all, the thousands of lawyers assisting companies in antitrust advice are in need for clear precedents.

Some common procedural standards could flow in future still from ECJ judgments, both relating to the principle of *"effectiveness"* – as argued by the Commission in its Staff Working Document and accompanying Communication- but also to a common respect for fundamental procedural right across the EU. However, arguably and in the interest of a more rapid clarification, progress should ideally come through progressive harmonisation of laws within the ECN, possibly even through EU legislative acts.[72] Indeed, as stressed by the Commission itself,[73] it is clear that convergence cannot always be achieved by more soft tools.

---

[72] In the same way as already done by the legislation in the EU directive or damages for branch of competition rule.

[73] See above quoted communication by the Commission to the European Parliament and the Council, Doc. COM (2014) 453, at § 33.

PART II: POWER TO ISSUE POSITIVE DECISIONS; POWER TO ADOPT COMMITMENT DECISIONS AND TO IMPOSE FINES FOR NON-COMPLIANCE WITH COMMITMENTS; POWER TO ADOPT REMEDIES, STRUCTURAL OR BEHAVIOURAL[*]

■

Mario Siragusa and Alessandro Bardanzellu

I. Introduction

Council Regulation (EC) No. 1/2003 ("Regulation 1/2003")[1] introduces a new legislative framework for the enforcement of competition rules in the European Union ("EU"). This new framework is based on the full direct applicability of such rules both in the EU and at the national level. At the same time, this framework has greatly enhanced the role of national competition authorities ("NCAs") and national courts as enforcers of EU competition rules.[2]

Looking back at the first ten years of implementation of Regulation 1/2003, it appears clear that it was a true legislative key stone in the enforcement of antitrust policy, both at the EU and national level, especially in a decade characterized by significant changes in the competitive scenario. In fact,

---

[*] This paper represents an updated and extended version of a presentation given by Mario Siragusa during the 10th Annual Conference of the GCLC: "The Ten Years of Regulation 1/2003: Procedural convergence and other outstanding issues to increase Coherence and Effectiveness, held in Brussels on November 6-7, 2014.

[1] Council Regulation (EC) No. 1/2003 of 16 December 2002 on the implementation of the rules on competition laid down in Articles 81 and 82 of the Treaty, OJ L 1, 04.01.2003, pp. 1-25.

[2] See, e.g., Recital 6 ("[i]n order to ensure that the Community competition rules are applied effectively, the competition authorities of the Member States should be associated more closely with their application. To this end, they should be empowered to apply Community law") and Recital 7 of Regulation 1/2003 ("[n]ational courts have an essential part to play in applying the Community competition rules. When deciding disputes between private individuals, they protect the subjective rights under Community law, for example by awarding damages to the victims of infringements. The role of the national courts here complements that of the competition authorities of the Member States. They should therefore be allowed to apply Articles 81 and 82 of the Treaty in full").

since May 1, 2004 (when Regulation 1/2003 entered into force), not only did thirteen new Member States join the EU, but also new technologies emerged and markets evolved, becoming more sophisticated and requiring more in-depth assessments by the EU Commission ("Commission") and NCAs. Moreover, the financial crisis pervaded recent years. In the EU, enhancement of competition law enforcement has been considered a part of the solution to the crisis, and has led to increased activities by antitrust authorities, more fiercely called to regulate the markets by sanctioning serious competition law infringements, and favoring liberalization processes through the removal of obstacles impairing effective competition.

In this scenario, Regulation 1/2003 has served as an efficient tool to increasing convergence in antitrust enforcement, by favoring a uniform application of EU competition rules at the national level.[3] More specifically, the decision-making powers granted by Regulation 1/2003 allows the Commission and NCAs to continue developing and enforcing an effective and harmonized competition policy throughout the EU. To this end, Regulation 1/2003 also introduces a set of procedural tools, aimed at ensuring consistency in the decisional practice of NCAs, as well as an adequate level of coordination between their initiatives.[4] In this new legislative framework, characterized by the repeal of the system of notification set forth by former Regulation No. 17/62,[5] and the consequent increase of the Commission's "prosecutorial" prerogatives, the latter has continued exercising a prominent and leading enforcer role, which also includes supervising NCAs' enforcement activities.

However, the pervasive decision-making powers of Regulation 1/2003 have not been fully exploited to date. Indeed, some actions can still be taken, at the EU and national level, in order to achieve a greater degree of

---

[3] See G. MONTI, *Independence, Interdependence, and Legitimacy: The EU Commission, National Competition Authorities, and the European Competition Network*, EUI Working Papers, LAW 2014/01, p. 15, available online at http://ssrn.com/abstract=2379320.

[4] See M. SIRAGUSA and G. FAELLA, *The Implementation of Competition Rules in the Two Years since Modernization*, in European Antitrust between EC Law and National Law (European Lawyers' Union 5th Symposium, Treviso, Italy), Giuffré, Milan, 2007, p. 2.

[5] *EEC Council: Regulation No. 17: First Regulation implementing Articles 85 and 86 of the Treaty*, OJ 013, 21.02.1962, pp. 204-211. Regulation 1/2003 explicitly recognizes the Commission's different role in "modernized" EU competition law, clarifying that "[t]*he centralised scheme set up by Regulation No. 17 no longer secures a balance between those two objectives* [*i.e.*, the need to ensure effective supervision and to simplify administration to the greatest possible extent]. *It hampers application of the Community competition rules by the courts and competition authorities of the Member States, and the system of notification it involves prevents the Commission from concentrating its resources on curbing the most serious infringements. It also imposes considerable costs on undertakings*" (Recital 3).

convergence both from a procedural and substantive standpoint. In particular, an effort to overcome national differences still existing in Member States' competition law systems would contribute to strengthening an already effective enforcement system within the EU, under the direction and supervision of the Commission.

The present paper will provide a brief outlook of some of the decision-making powers afforded by Regulation 1/2003, and discuss the current state of convergence. In particular, the power to issue positive decisions (*infra*, *sub* 2), the power to adopt commitment decisions and to impose fines for non-compliance with commitments (*infra*, *sub* 3), and the power to adopt remedies, structural or behavioural (*infra*, *sub* 4) will, in turn, be considered. At the same time, the paper will emphasize procedural and substantive divergences in the Member States' enforcement policies, which still impair the achievement of a fully coherent competition law system within the EU.

II. Power to Issue Positive Decisions

Regulation 1/2003 sets forth two different types of "positive decisions", which can be adopted by the Commission and the NCAs, respectively.[6]

While such positive decisions could in principle represent a powerful legal tool to promote a uniform application of EU competition law, thus increasing convergence, it must be acknowledged that, in practice, they had little (*rectius*, zero) success thus far. As shown *infra*, the lack of positive decisions seems to be in contrast to the guidance role that Regulation 1/2003 conferred to the Commission.

A. Art. 10 of Regulation 1/2003

As a mean to clarify EU competition law and ensure its consistent application throughout the EU, Art. 10 of Regulation 1/2003 grants the Commission the power to adopt "positive" decisions "*of a declaratory nature*" finding the inapplicability of Art. 101 or Art. 102 of the Treaty of the Functioning of the European Union ("TFEU"), "*where the interest of the Community so requires*".[7] Pursuant to Art. 10, the Commission can also ascertain that, even if an agreement or practice violates *prima facie* Art. 101(1) TFEU,

---

[6]   See Art. 10 and Art. 5 of Regulation 1/2003.
[7]   See Recital 14 of Regulation 1/2003.

it can still meet the conditions for an individual exemption set forth in Art. 101(3) TFEU.

The rationale behind Art. 10 clearly lies with the principle of legal certainty. It is in the interest and benefit of undertakings to know with certainty if their conduct is compliant with competition law. Indeed, Regulation 1/2003 explicitly recognized the role of legal certainty in the application of EU competition law with the ultimate goal of promoting innovation and investment.[8] Similarly, Regulation 1/2003 encourages individual undertakings to seek informal guidance from the Commission as regards cases giving rise *"to genuine uncertainty because they present novel or unresolved questions for the application"* of EU competition law.[9]

Art. 10 of Regulation 1/2003, thus, emphasizes the central role of the Commission in the enforcement of competition law, which is enhanced by Art. 16 of same, pursuant to which all Commission decisions (including, of course, positive decisions) are binding on NCAs and national courts. The latter cannot take any decisions running counter to those adopted by the Commission. Based on this, it can be easily argued that in the "modernized" legal framework introduced by Regulation 1/2003 (and notwithstanding the direct applicability of EU competition law and the legislative efforts to concentrate the Commission's enforcement activities on the most serious competition law infringements), the EU legislators still wished to preserve some of the previous "supervisory" prerogatives of the Commission to ensure a uniform application of Art. 101 and Art. 102 TFEU.

That said, one cannot avoid mentioning certain limits and inconsistencies in the enforcement of EU competition law, especially with respect to positive decisions, which can affect the coherence of the entire system. First of all, recourse to Art. 10 is limited to *"exceptional cases"*,[10] *e.g.*, when it is necessary to clarify the law and ensure its consistent application throughout the EU.[11] In particular, the applicability of Art. 10 is subject to two cumulative conditions: (i) the Commission must act *"on its own initiative"*[12]

---

[8]   See Recital 38 of Regulation 1/2003.
[9]   *Ibid.*
[10] See Recital 14 of Regulation 1/2003.
[11] See the *Commission Staff Working Document "Ten Years of Antitrust Enforcement under Regulation 1/2003"*, SWD (2014) 230 final, § 193. Moreover, based on the Antitrust Manual of Procedures, an Art. 10 decision is needed to avoid or resolve a problem of coherence resulting from divergent interpretations by national courts in different Member States or by members of the ECN (see *Antitrust Manual of Procedures, Internal DG Competition working documents on procedures for the application of Articles 101 and 102 TFEU*, March 2012, Module 18, § 1. See also, in this sense, L. ORTIZ BLANCO (ed.), *EU Competition Procedure*, Oxford, Oxford University Press, 2013, 3rd edition, p. 597).
[12] See Art. 10 of Regulation 1/2003.

and (ii) it must intervene only when the *"Community public interest* [...] *so requires".* From a practical perspective, the cumulative nature of these two conditions excessively restricts the scope of application of Art. 10. In fact, the Commission cannot act in the pure interests of individual undertakings.[13] Moreover, given that Regulation 1/2003 abolishes the centralised notification and authorisation system, the Commission has currently limited exposure to detect cases which may require an intervention under Art. 10.

It is thus not surprising that no Art. 10 decisions have been adopted to date by the Commission.

B. Art. 5 of Regulation 1/2003

Art. 5 of Regulation 1/2003 grants NCAs the power to apply Art. 101 and Art. 102 TFEU in individual cases, and to adopt positive decisions, concluding that *"there are no grounds for action on their part"*, where, *"on the basis of the information in their possession the conditions for prohibitions are not met".* Almost all Member States' jurisdictions currently include a specific provision allowing the NCA to adopt this type of positive decision at the end of an Art. 101 or Art. 102 TFEU investigation.[14]

However, there is a significant difference between positive decisions that the Commission may adopt pursuant to Art. 10 of Regulation 1/2003 and those envisaged by Art. 5.

In *Tele2 Polska*,[15] the European Court of Justice ("ECJ") clarified that, even though NCAs could directly apply EU competition law provisions, only the Commission is empowered to conclude that there had been no breach of such provisions (the so-called finding of inapplicability, pursuant to Art. 10 of Regulation 1/2003). Therefore, when a NCA concludes that no antitrust infringement occurred, it can only rule that there are "no grounds for action" on its part. This conclusion, however, does not signify that the conduct under investigation *fully* complies with EU competition law.

Therefore, within its general goal to ensure a consistent application of EU competition law, Regulation 1/2003 (as further interpreted by the ECJ) basically grants the Commission the *exclusive* power to adopt positive

---

[13] See the *Commission Staff Working Document,* SWD (2014) 230 final, cited above, § 193.
[14] See the *Decision-Making Powers Report adopted* by the ECN Working Group Cooperation Issues and Due Process, 31 October 2012, pp. 36-37, available online at http://ec.europa.eu/competition/ecn/decision_making_powers_report_en.pdf.
[15] See Case C-375/09, *Tele2 Polska sp,* [2011] ECR, p. I-3055.

decisions on the *non-applicability* of EU competition law provisions to certain practices. It thus seems clear that EU legislators wished to prevent NCAs from adopting "fully positive" decisions which could bind the Commission, other NCAs and national courts and could be used to block enforcement in other Member States.[16] This results in a clear unbalance in NCAs' enforcement powers: they can fully apply EU competition law when adopting infringement decisions, but they are prevented from doing so when no violations have occurred.

From the standpoint of procedural convergence, the interpretation of Art. 5 given by the ECJ in *Tele2 Polska* could raise doubts. In fact, even though Regulation 1/2003 specifies that the Commission and NCAs "*should form together a network of public authorities applying the Community competition rules in close cooperation*",[17] it significantly differentiates the enforcement powers granted to the former *vis-à-vis* the latter with respect to the adoption of positive decisions.

Moreover, the aforementioned interpretation seems to sit uneasily with the new central role played by NCAs in the enforcement of EU competition law, as provided in the recent Directive on Antitrust Damages. Similar to Art. 16 of Regulation 1/2003, the Directive recognizes that "*an infringement of competition law found by a final decision of a national competition authority or a review court is deemed to be irrefutably established for the purposes of an action for damages brought before their national courts*".[18]

Considering the above, one may wonder if the possibility for NCAs to adopt decisions finding the inapplicability of Art. 101 or Art. 102 TFEU would really "*call into question the system of cooperation established*"[19] by Regulation 1/2003 or, conversely, it would contribute to increasing effectiveness in the enforcement of EU competition law.

---

[16] See the *Commission Staff Working Document*, SWD (2014) 230 final, cited above, § 198. See also Case C-375/09, *Tele2 Polska sp*, cited above, §§ 27-28: "[e]*mpowerment of national competition authorities to take decisions stating that there has been no breach of Article 102 TFEU would call into question the system of cooperation established by the Regulation and would undermine the power of the Commission [...], since such a decision might prevent the Commission from finding subsequently that the practice in question amounts to a breach of those provisions of European Union Law*".

[17] See Recital 15 of Regulation 1/2003.

[18] See Article 9 of *Directive 2014/104/EU of the European Parliament and of the Council of 26 November 2014 on certain rules governing actions for damages under national law for infringements of the competition law provisions of the Member States and of the European Union, OJ* L 349, 5.12.2014, pp. 1-19.

[19] See Case C-375/09, *Tele2 Polska sp*, cited above, § 27.

Supporters of the *Tele2 Polska* ruling may believe that granting NCAs the power to adopt "fully positive" decisions would *"undermine the power of the Commission"*[20] and possibly lead to national decisions in contrast with established EU competition law principles. However, this potential disruptive scenario could be avoided by enhancing the Commission's powers in the context of Art. 5 decisions. For instance, the EU legislators could intervene in the legal framework established by Regulation 1/2003 and require NCAs to (i) inform the Commission also before the adoption of positive decisions (similar to what is already set forth by Art. 11(4) of Regulation 1/2003 for infringement and commitment decisions[21]) and (ii) grant the Commission the power to intervene and block the adoption of such decisions when they appear to be in contrast with EU competition law. This legislative intervention – together with an amendment of Art. 5 of Regulation 1/2003 granting NCAs the power to adopt decisions finding the inapplicability of Art. 101 or Art. 102 TFEU – could still ensure a uniform application of EU competition law, without depriving NCAs of the power to enforce effectively the provisions of the Treaty also through the adoption of "fully positive" decisions.

Finally, the fact that NCAs are currently only empowered to adopt "no ground for actions" decisions could in principle duplicate competition law proceedings in connection with the same conduct. In particular, even if an NCA previously closed an investigation because it found that the undertakings involved did not commit any violation, the Commission would not be prevented from subsequently initiating proceedings in connection with the same conduct. This possibility may be seen as running counter to at least the principle of procedural economy, if not with the principle of *ne bis in idem*.

---

[20] *Ibid.*

[21] Pursuant to Art. 11(4) of Regulation 1/2003, "[n]o *later than 30 days before the adoption of a decision requiring that an infringement be brought to an end, accepting commitments or withdrawing the benefit of a block exemption Regulation, the competition authorities of the Member States shall inform the Commission. To that effect, they shall provide the Commission with a summary of the case, the envisaged decision or, in the absence thereof, any other document indicating the proposed course of action. This information may also be made available to the competition authorities of the other Member States. At the request of the Commission, the acting competition authority shall make available to the Commission other documents it holds which are necessary for the assessment of the case. The information supplied to the Commission may be made available to the competition authorities of the other Member States. National competition authorities may also exchange between themselves information necessary for the assessment of a case that they are dealing with under Article 81 or Article 82 of the Treaty"*.

C. Consequences and Future Perspectives

Due to the legislative framework illustrated above, and, particularly, the stringent requirements for the application of Art. 10 of Regulation 1/2003 and the limited scope of Art. 5, positive decisions do not seem to constitute currently an effective legal tool to enhance coherence in the enforcement of EU competition law.

In the first ten years of application of Regulation 1/2003, the decisional practice of the Commission focused mostly on antitrust violations (*i.e.*, nearly all of the decisions adopted by the Commission ascertained violations of Art. 101 and/or Art. 102 TFEU) and not even one positive decision was issued. The Commission's leading position in the application of EU competition law has shifted towards a sort of *ex ante* regulatory role, as demonstrated by the numerous Guidelines adopted following Regulation 1/2003.

These soft law instruments provide an analytical framework based on legal and economic criteria (stemming from the decisional practice of the Commission and the case law of the EU courts) that help undertakings carry out their own assessment under EU competition law. By regulating various legal issues arising in the application of Art. 101 and Art. 102 TFEU, the Guidelines have certainly contributed to the development of competition law within the EU.

However, especially with respect to the application of Art. 101(3) TFEU, the extensive use of soft law instruments has not been effectively supplemented by adequate case law, in particular by the adoption of positive decisions, which could have ensured a comprehensive enforcement of EU competition law through a continuous interpretation and application of the principles enshrined in the Guidelines.[22] In particular, positive decisions could have: (i) addressed particular (or new) legal issues not covered by the Guidelines (thus, developing EU competition law on a continuous basis); and (ii) provided legal certainty to undertakings which request the Commission to specifically address such issues.

---

[22] This is even more true with respect those Guidelines that were adopted right after the entry into force of Regulation 1/2003 and have not yet been replaced by more recent acts. For instance, scholars question if the Commission's Guidelines on the application of Art. 101(3) TFEU still represent an efficient tool to ensure coherence in the enforcement of EU competition law provisions. In fact, they date back to 2004 and, thus, do not take into account recent developments which occurred (especially) in emerging markets (see N. PETIT, *The Guidelines on the Application of Article 81(3) EC – A Critical Review*, Working Paper Institut d'Études Juridiques Europeennes (IEJE) No. 4/2009, available online at http://ssrn.com/abstract=1428558).

As mentioned, Art. 1 of Regulation 1/2003 abolishes the system of notification and exemptions introduced by Regulation 17/1962, thus requiring undertakings to self-assess whether their arrangements comply with EU competition law. Therefore, whereas, in the old regime, Art. 101(3) had a crucial role in shaping competition law policy in the EU, now it is directly applied by undertakings, without any *ex ante* intervention by the Commission. This lack of application of Art. 101(3) TFEU in the Commission's decisional practice[23] does not seem to be in line with the effect-based approach at the basis of the modernization of the EU competition law system.

Accordingly, a broader scope of intervention by the Commission – the only competition authority in the EU entrusted with the power to adopt "fully positive" decisions – to clarify when a conduct does not qualify as a competition law violation, or, in the alternative, when it meets the conditions set forth in Art. 101(3) TFEU, would have supplemented the soft law framework established following Regulation 1/2003 and contributed to promoting a more harmonious application of competition law throughout the EU to the benefit of legal certainty.

Such conclusion is even more true in light of the significant changes which have occurred since 2004. Following the introduction of Regulation 1/2003, the number of EU Member States almost doubled. At the same time, new markets and technologies emerged, and private enforcement significantly developed throughout the EU. Also in light of these circumstances, we believe that the Commission still needs to play an effective leading role in the EU competition law arena. The increase in the number of NCAs translates into a stronger need for convergence, to ensure a uniform application of competition law principles throughout the EU. New markets and technologies entail more sophisticated competition law analysis; potential anticompetitive concerns need to be identified and efficiencies must be weighed, with the ultimate goal of consumer benefit. Finally, the growth of private enforcement has led to a more frequent direct application of Art. 101 and Art. 102 TFEU by national judges, which typically have less competition law experience than the Commission (and EU courts). Therefore, more guidance (*i.e.*, case law) would be desirable to ensure a

---

[23] In recent years, the Commission carried out a detailed assessment under Art. 101(3) TFEU in only a few cases: see, *e.g.*, Commission decisions (i) of December 19, 2007, Cases COMP/34.579, *MasterCard*; COMP/36.518, *EuroCommerce*; and COMP/38.580, *Commercial Cards*; and (ii) of July 16, 2003, Case COMP/38.369, *T Mobile Deutschland/O2 Germany: Network Sharing Rahmenvertrag*. An assessment under Art. 101(3) was also carried out in the Commission decision of May 23, 2013, Case COMP/AT.39595, *Continental/United/Lufthansa/Air Canada*.

consistent application of EU competition law also in the field of private enforcement.

There is no doubt that the Commission is still the best-placed entity capable of enhancing coherence and effectiveness in the uniform enforcement of competition law, and that its "positive" guidance role can contribute to boosting "a competition law culture" in the EU. The hope is that in the near future, the Commission will start exercising its power to adopt positive decisions pursuant to Art. 10 of Regulation 1/2003 also with the aim of revitalizing Art. 101(3) TFEU.

III. Power to Adopt Commitment Decisions and to Impose Fines for Non-Compliance with Commitments

A. Commitment Decisions

Art. 9 of Regulation 1/2003 grants the Commission the power to accept commitments offered by undertakings subject to an Art. 101 or Art. 102 TFEU investigation, to make them binding and to close proceedings without ascertaining any infringements. Pursuant to Art. 5 of Regulation 1/2003, a similar power to accept commitments is also granted to NCAs.

Commitments allow the Commission (and NCAs) to save resources and time for (more serious) infringements that may require the imposition of a pecuniary fine. In fact, pursuant to Recital 13 of Regulation 1/2003, commitment decisions are not appropriate in case of serious infringements, *i.e.*, when the Commission deems it opportune to impose a fine.[24]

---

[24] Notably, Recital 13 also provides that commitment decisions *"are without prejudice to the powers of competition authorities and courts of the Member States to make such a finding and decide upon the case"*. Furthermore, Recital 22 clarifies that *"commitment decisions adopted by the Commission do not affect the power of the courts and the competition authorities of the Member States to apply Articles 101 and 102 TFEU"*. A potential risk of divergence between, on the one hand, Commission commitment decisions and, on the other hand, national court judgments or NCA decisions, asserted by some scholars never arose in practice. In any case, most scholars believe that Art. 16(2) of Regulation 1/2003 would prevent national courts or NCAs from adopting decisions conflicting with a Commission commitment decision addressing the same facts. See, in this sense, H. SCHWEITZER, *Commitment Decisions under Art. 9 of Regulation 1/2003: The Developing EC Practice and Case Law*, EUI Working Papers, LAW 2008/22, pp. 24-26, available online at http://papers.ssrn.com/sol3/papers.cfm?abstract_id=1306245, and F. WAGNER-VON PAPP, "Best and even better practices in commitment procedures after Alrosa: The dangers of abandoning the 'struggle for competition law'", in *Common Market Law Review*, 2012, 49, issue 3, pp. 952 *et seq.* See also the *Commission Staff Working Paper*, SEC (2009) 574 final, cited above, §§ 107-108.

Commitments have played a relevant role in the enforcement practice of both the Commission and NCAs. From May 2004 to December 2013, the Commission adopted 33 commitment decisions under Art. 9 of Regulation 1/2003.[25] In these decisions, the Commission accepted both behavioural and structural commitments. At the national level, commitment decisions adopted by NCAs accounted for 23% of all envisaged decisions submitted by the NCAs to the Commission, pursuant to Art. 11(4) of Regulation 1/2003,[26] from May 2004 to December 2013.[27]

Currently, all NCAs have the discretional power (*i.e.*, they are not obliged) to accept commitments voluntarily offered by undertakings.[28] This represents a clear and commendable example of full convergence between Member States.[29] However, both at the EU and national level, full convergence still does not exist as to when (*i.e.*, in which cases) the adoption of a commitment decision would be appropriate. As noted above, at the EU level, Recital 13 of Regulation 1/2003 states that commitment decisions are not appropriate in cases where the Commission intends to impose a fine. In such cases, the need to punish the undertaking's conduct and to impose a sanction with a deterrent effect prevails over the possibility to close proceedings by accepting the commitments offered by the concerned undertaking.

At the national level, the principle set forth in Recital 13 has been generally recognized. In particular, in most jurisdictions, most of the serious competition law infringements are *a priori* excluded from the scope of application of commitment decisions.[30]

However, to date, with the exception of cartels (*i.e.*, Art. 101 TFEU hardcore restrictions), full convergence does not still exist as to what constitutes "serious infringements". More specifically, some jurisdictions merely recall the principle set forth in Recital 13 and generally exclude the applicability of commitments when a prohibition decision (*e.g.*, Spain and

---

[25] See the *Commission Staff Working Document*, SWD (2014) 230 final, cited above, § 186.

[26] See above, footnote No. 21.

[27] See the *Commission Staff Working Document*, SWD (2014) 230 final, cited above, § 196.

[28] As a further update to the *Decision-Making Powers Report* of October 31, 2012 of the *ECN Working Group Cooperation Issues and Due Process*, cited above, it seems that also in Estonia the local NCA was granted the power to accept commitments.

[29] Commitment decisions constitute "*a prime example of procedural convergence based on inspiration from the EU model and the cross-fertilisation of ideas supported by multilateral cooperation*": see the *Commission Staff Working Document*, SWD(2014) 230 final, cited above, § 196.

[30] See the *Decision-Making Powers Report* adopted by the ECN Working Group Cooperation Issues and Due Process, cited above, p. 29.

Sweden) or the imposition of a fine (*e.g.*, Germany and Denmark) is deemed appropriate. Other jurisdictions explicitly exclude from commitment decisions also: (i) the most serious abuses of dominant position (*e.g.*, Bulgaria, France and the UK); (ii) infringements that already produced effects (*e.g.*, Czech Republic, Spain); (iii) infringements whose aim is to restrict competition (*e.g.*, the Netherlands).[31]

Based on the above, most NCAs (as well as the Commission) are granted broad discretion in identifying cases in which the adoption of a commitment decision is appropriate. This legal uncertainty can potentially lead to an exploitation of the commitment procedure by competition authorities, which may force, under the threat of a heavy fine, concerned undertakings to offer commitments even in cases where no clear or serious (*prima facie*) competition law violation had occurred. Therefore, in these cases, commitments would be an undertaking's only choice to avoid the risk of a fine, rather than constituting a direct up-front remedy to resolve the alleged anticompetitive concerns.

And there is still more. Pursuant to Recital 13 of Regulation 1/2003, the dichotomy commitment *vis-à-vis* heavy fine should be avoided in principle. In fact, proceedings where an undertaking is potentially exposed to a fine (*i.e.*, proceedings in connection with serious antitrust violations), are not candidates *ex lege* for a commitment decision. Conversely, commitments constitute a valid legal tool only when they meet the preliminary concerns of the competition authorities and no longer render opportune any further action.

The above shows that clearly identifying what cases could be (at least in principle) closed through the adoption of commitment decisions would ensure substantial convergence both at the EU and national level and would avoid exploitative or contradictory uses of commitments.

The substantial assessment of commitments offered by undertakings also raises some convergence issues. In general, as laid down in Art. 9 of Regulation 1/2003, commitments should be accepted if they meet the *prima facie* competition concerns raised by competition authorities. As clarified in *Alrosa*,[32] the principle of proportionality in the context of Art. 9 of Regulation 1/2003 requires the Commission only to verify "*that the commitments in question address the concerns it expressed to the undertakings concerned and that they have not offered less onerous commitments*

---

[31] See the *Decision-Making Powers Report* adopted by the ECN Working Group Cooperation Issues and Due Process, cited above, p. 30.

[32] See Case C-441/07, *Commission v. Alrosa*, [2010] ECR, p. I-5949.

that also address those concerns adequately".[33] The Commission is thus not obliged to seek out less onerous solutions, and the relative burden is placed upon the undertaking. This means that the scope of application of the proportionality principle in commitment proceedings is quite limited and the Commission enjoys broad discretion in the substantial assessment of commitments.

In *Alrosa*, however, there was no mention of the criteria that the Commission should, in practice, use when assessing a commitment's ability to meet competition concerns. This lack of guidance and the consequent discretion and flexibility that competition authorities enjoy when evaluating commitments still prevent full convergence and facilitate conflicting interpretations at the national level.[34]

Finally, Regulation 1/2003 does not govern the procedures for the adoption of commitment decisions, which are typically devolved to the national regimes. A quick overview reveals that further convergence would be desirable in certain areas to harmonize national procedures and avoid inconsistencies.

More specifically, in most jurisdictions, similarly to the EU system,[35] there is no procedural time limit for offering commitments (see, *e.g.*, Germany, Belgium, the UK, *etc.*).[36] Other EU Member States introduced specific time-frames in which to present commitments. For instance, in France, commitments can be offered only before the adoption of the Statement of Objections ("SO"), while in Slovenia they can be offered only before the

---

[33] *Ibid.*, § 41.

[34] For instance, in Italy, the Regional Administrative Tribunal (*"TAR Lazio"*) recently adopted a rather stringent (and innovative) approach to assessing commitments offered by an undertaking subject to an abuse of dominance proceedings and held that commitments could not be accepted in connection with a conduct that already produced its (allegedly) anticompetitive effects, unless such commitments could retroactively remove these effects (see the judgment of the *TAR Lazio* No. 3964/2011, *Conto TV v. Autorità Garante della Concorrenza e del Mercato*). However, on appeal, the judgment was annulled by the Supreme Administrative Court (*"Consiglio di Stato"*), which adopted a different (and, probably, *"more traditional"*) approach. The Court clarified that the commitments' ability to cure the anticompetitive effects already produced by the contested conduct was not an essential requirement, the lack of which prevents the Italian Competition Authority ("ICA") from accepting the commitments and closing the investigation without ascertaining any infringement (see the judgment of the *Consiglio di Stato* No. 4773/2014, *Autorità Garante della Concorrenza e del Mercato v. Conto TV*).

[35] See, *e.g.*, the Commission decision of September 29, 2010, Case COMP/39.315, *ENI*, in which commitments were offered to the Commission after the hearing.

[36] For instance, in the Netherlands an application for commitment decision may be filed until an infringement decision has been adopted. See, in this sense, the *Decision-Making Powers Report* adopted by the ECN Working Group Cooperation Issues and Due Process, cited above, p. 30.

expiry of the deadline for submitting a reply to the SO. In Greece, a proposal for commitment cannot be made at a late stage of the procedure. In the Czech Republic, a commitment proposal may be presented only after the adoption of the SO. In Italy, Art. 14-*ter* of Law No. 287/90 requires companies to offer commitments within three months from the notification of the decision opening the investigation.[37]

More convergence would be desirable in connection with procedural time limits for offering commitments set forth at the national level. This is even more true in cases where an undertaking is subject to parallel investigations in more than one national jurisdictions (*e.g.*, in Germany and Italy). In those cases, the possibility to offer commitments to an NCA in the early stage of the investigation only (*e.g.*, in Italy), while being free to do that in any phase of the (parallel) proceeding before another NCA (*e.g.*, in Germany) might jeopardize the overall defensive strategies of an undertaking and certainly not favor an uniform application of EU competition law.[38]

B. Fines for Non-Compliance with Commitments

In case of non-compliance with commitments, Art. 23(2)(c) of Regulation 1/2003 provides that the Commission may impose a fine on the undertaking concerned. This fine can run up to 10% of the undertaking's total turnover in the preceding business year.

Notably, the 10% cap is equal to the cap imposed in case of Art. 7 decisions, *i.e.*, in case of a decision finding a competition law infringement (see *infra*). This choice of EU legislators has raised the question whether the

---

[37] However, the Italian courts clarified that the three-month deadline did not have a preclusive or mandatory nature and could be departed from based on a case-by-case analysis (see the recent judgment of the *Consiglio di Stato* No. 4773/2014, *Autorità Garante della Concorrenza e del Mercato v. Conto TV*, cited above). Moreover, the ICA, in its guidelines on the application of Art. 14-*ter* of Law No. 287/90 clarified that, in exceptional cases, and on the basis of a justified and timely request of a party, commitments offered after the expiry of the three-month deadline could still be accepted.

[38] According to M. Siragusa and G. Faella, *The Implementation of Competition Rules in the Two Years since Modernization*, cited above, p. 19, "*an interpretation obliging firms to offer commitments in the early phase of the proceedings, before a preliminary assessment has been issued and parties have had enough time to adequately evaluate the appropriate measures to be proposed, would seriously prejudice the due process right of the companies concerned, as they could offer more than they need to. Furthermore, even when proceedings are already in an advanced phase, commitment decisions may allow the achievement of objectives pursued by Articles 5 and 9 of Reg. 1/2003, i.e. the termination and/or prevention of potentially anticompetitive conduct and the saving of administrative costs*".

10% cap in case of sanctions for non-compliance with commitments should be reduced for proportionality reasons.[39]

In addition, the Commission has never clarified what the applicable criteria are to be taken into account when imposing fines for non-compliance with commitments, considering also that the Commission's Fining Guidelines are not applicable in this case.[40]

To date, the Commission has adopted only one Art. 23(2)(c) decision in the *Microsoft* saga,[41] where it imposed a fine of EUR 561 million, equal to 1.02% of Microsoft's turnover.

Pursuant to Art. 24(1)(c) of Regulation 1/2003, the Commission may also impose periodic penalty payments (not exceeding 5% of the average daily turnover in the preceding business year) to compel undertakings to comply with commitments made binding by an Art. 9 decision. To date, however, this provision has never been applied.

Convergence in connection with the powers granted to NCAs to ensure compliance with commitments has not been fully achieved at the national level. There are still some NCAs (namely, the Estonian, Greek, Irish, Latvian, Lithuanian and British authorities) that have no power to impose fines for non-compliance with commitments. Such divergence shows that some NCAs are better equipped than others, and are fully empowered to ensure enforcement of – and compliance with – commitments.[42]

In conclusion, more convergence should be achieved in relation to the powers granted to NCAs in case of parties' non-compliance with commitment decisions, in terms of (i) effective competence to impose pecuniary fines and (ii) consistent principles and guidelines in calculating such fines.

IV. Power to Adopt Remedies, Structural or Behavioural

The power to impose remedies is an important tool to bring infringements to an end, prevent their recurrence and restore competition in the

---

[39] See, *e.g.*, L. Ortiz Blanco (ed.), *EU Competition Procedure*, cited above, p. 590, who proposed a cap equal to 1% of the undertaking's total turnover in the preceding business year.

[40] *Guidelines on the method of setting fines imposed pursuant to Article 23(2)(a) of Regulation No. 1/2003*, OJ C 210, 1.9.2006, pp. 2-5.

[41] See the Commission decision of March 6, 2013, Case COMP/39.530, *Microsoft (Tying)*.

[42] The adoption of effective sanctions in case of non-compliance with commitments is also advised by the *ECN Recommendation on Commitment Procedures*, December 2013, § 23, available online at http://ec.europa.eu/competition/ecn/ecn_recommendation_commitments_09122013_en.pdf.

market.[43] In particular, Art. 7 of Regulation 1/2003 entitles the Commission to impose, in the context of a prohibition decision, *"any behavioural or structural remedies which are proportionate to the infringement committed and necessary to bring the infringement effectively to an end"*.

As clearly stated in Art. 7, in imposing remedies, the Commission must comply with the principle of proportionality, in order to avoid imposing remedies which go beyond what is required to terminate an infringement and restore competitive conditions in the affected market.[44] To this end, Art. 7 and Recital 12 of Regulation 1/2003 establish a sort of hierarchy between behavioural and structural remedies. In particular, *"structural remedies should only be imposed either where there is no equally effective behavioural remedy or where any equally effective behavioural remedy would be more burdensome for the undertaking concerned than the structural remedy. Changes to the structure of an undertaking as it existed before the infringement was committed would only be proportionate where there is a substantial risk of a lasting or repeated infringement that derives from the very structure of the undertaking"*.[45]

The stringent proportionality test reduces the scope of applicability of structural remedies under Art. 7 of Regulation 1/2003. Scholars generally agree with this approach, since a measure entailing a permanent change in the structure of an undertaking is far more intrusive than a measure merely regulating its behavioural conduct.[46] Structural remedies are in fact considered an *extrema ratio* compared to behavioural ones.

This approach significantly differentiates remedies imposed in the framework of Art. 7 from those adopted in the context of merger control proceedings, where structural remedies are normally considered the most

---

[43] See the *Commission Staff Working Document "Enhancing Competition Enforcement by the Member States' Competition Authorities: Institutional and Procedural issues"*, SWD (2014) 231 final, § 59.

[44] From this standpoint, the proportionality test applicable in case of Art. 7 decisions is more extended than in case of commitment decisions (Art. 9 decisions), since, in the former case, the Commission is constrained by the limits of the "equally effective/less burdensome remedy", which – as clarified in *Alrosa* – are not applicable in the framework of commitment proceedings. See also W. WANG, *Structural Remedies in EU Antitrust and Merger Control*, in *World Competition* 34, No. 4 (2011), pp. 585-587.

[45] See Recital 12 of Regulation 1/2003. The same provision is included in Art. 7, pursuant to which *"structural remedies can only be imposed either where there is no equally effective behavioural remedy or where any equally effective behavioural remedy would be more burdensome for the undertaking concerned than the structural remedy"*.

[46] See L. ORTIZ BLANCO (ed.), *EU Competition Procedure*, cited above, p. 471; W. WANG, *Structural Remedies in EU Antitrust and Merger Control*, cited above, p. 587.

effective tool to ensure that a proposed concentration does not substantially lessen competition.

On the contrary, structural remedies can be imposed in the context of a prohibition decision only when there is a close link between the structure of the concerned undertaking(s) and the sanctioned infringement that creates the risk of a *"lasting or repeated"* competition law violation. In all other cases, the imposition of a structural remedy would go beyond the scope of a prohibition decision and, thus, violate the proportionality principle. This is the reason why, to date, in the framework of Art. 7 decisions, the Commission has imposed behavioural remedies only.[47]

From another standpoint, the different scope of application of the proportionality principle in the framework of Art. 7 and Art. 9 decisions likely explains why – contrary to prohibition decisions – structural measures have been frequently offered and accepted in commitment proceedings.[48] As noted *supra, sub* 3(a), commitments are proposed by the undertakings subject to an investigation, hypothetically under the possible threat of a heavy fine, which might induce them to offer a set of (structural) measures aimed at removing (or even potentially going beyond) the competition concerns preliminary identified by the competition authority. The *Alrosa* test, according to which the Commission is not obliged to look for less onerous solutions, is likely to ensure the compatibility of structural commitments with the proportionality principle also in case of subsequent judicial review, thus making the Commission more willing to accept structural measures in the framework of Art. 9 proceedings.

Conversely, structural remedies under Art. 7 of Regulation 1/2003 require the Commission's finding of an infringement and are directly imposed by the Commission itself, which has to prove their indispensability and respect the more stringent proportionality principle.[49]

Again, in the EU, there does not yet exist a full degree of convergence with respect to the powers to impose remedies in prohibition decisions granted

---

[47] See the *Commission Staff Working Document*, SWD (2014) 230 final, cited above, § 188. In particular, to date, behavioural remedies have been imposed in three Art. 7 decisions only: (i) decision of March 24, 2004, Case COMP/37.792, *Microsoft*; (ii) decision of December 19, 2007, Case COMP/34.579, *MasterCard*; and (iii) decision of July 16, 2008, Case COMP/38.698, *CISAC*. Most Art. 7 procedures were concluded with a cease and desist order.

[48] See, *e.g.*, the Commission decisions: (i) of November 26, 2008, Cases COMP/39.388-39.389, *E.ON*; (ii) of March 18, 2009, Case COMP/39.402, *RWE*; and (iii) of September 29, 2010, Case COMP/39.315, *ENI*, in which structural commitments were offered by the parties and accepted by the Commission.

[49] See W. Wang, *Structural Remedies in EU Antitrust and Merger Control*, cited above, pp. 585-587.

to NCAs. In particular, according to the relevant national legislations, the large majority of NCAs are explicitly entitled to impose both behavioural and structural remedies. In addition, similar to Art. 7 of Regulation 1/2003, in some jurisdictions (*e.g.*, Bulgaria, Spain, Malta), structural remedies may only be imposed where there is no behavioural remedy which would have an equivalent effect or where such behavioural remedy would be more onerous for the undertaking.

Even though, as just noted, the large majority of national systems are convergent with Regulation 1/2003, there are still a few NCAs which are allowed to adopt behavioural remedies only (*e.g.*, the Danish, Lithuanian and Swedish authorities) or are not granted with the power to impose remedies (*i.e.*, the Finnish, Polish and Slovakian authorities).

Finally, in some national jurisdictions, the power to impose remedies is not clearly spelled out. This is for instance the case in Italy, where Art. 15(1) of Law No. 287/90 only empowers the Italian Competition Authority ("ICA") to order the undertakings concerned to bring the infringement to an end within a certain term.[50] However, in practice, the ICA has exercised the prerogatives granted by Art. 15(1) above also to impose (behavioural and structural) remedies.

The overview above reveals a lack of convergence in (some of) the EU Member States' national systems. Full convergence at the national level would, in fact, strengthen legal certainty for undertakings, by limiting the risk of different treatment in case of parallel investigations in different jurisdictions (*e.g.*, in case of abuse of dominance proceedings, dominant undertakings may be currently exposed to structural remedies in some countries only).[51]

Accordingly, in those jurisdictions where full convergence with the EU system has not yet been achieved, national legislative provisions granting the NCAs the same power to impose remedies conferred to the Commission by Regulation 1/2003 would be desirable, also with the aim to limit the NCAs' discretion. Lacking an explicit and clear legislative framework, NCAs should exercise their power to impose behavioural and structural remedies (when granted) in an EU-oriented manner. In this respect, the

---

[50] See M. SIRAGUSA and G. FAELLA, "The Implementation of Competition Rules in the Two Years since Modernization", in *European Antitrust between EC Law and National Law* (European Lawyers' Union. 5th Symposium, Treviso, Italy), Giuffré, Milan, 2007, p. 19.

[51] See the *ECN Recommendation on the Power to Impose Structural Remedies*, December 2013, § 7, available online at http://ec.europa.eu/competition/ecn/structural_remedies_09122013_en.pdf.

role of national courts in the judicial review of NCAs' decisions is also crucial to enhancing coherence and effectiveness within the EU.

In particular, Italy constitutes a significant example of how national courts can shape the NCAs' use of remedies and increase convergence. As already noted, the ICA has no explicit power to impose remedies. However, the ICA has imposed both behavioural and structural remedies to undertakings in prohibition decisions.[52] The Italian administrative courts endorsed this practice, recognizing that the power to impose remedies in the context of infringement decisions is inherent to the role played by the ICA in the enforcement of competition rules at the national level.[53]

However, the lack of a provision explicitly granting the ICA the power to impose remedies also results in the absence of any explicit proportionality criterion in the choice of the remedy to be adopted. This led the ICA to impose structural remedies in prohibition decisions, without any assessment under the proportionality principle.[54] On appeal, however, the Italian administrative courts did not endorse the ICA's approach and annulled the decisions.[55] In these cases, as noted above, the judicial review of the national administrative courts was able to increase coherence between the EU and national systems in connection with the imposition of remedies in infringement decisions.

V. Final Remarks

Regulation 1/2003 has positively contributed to harmonizing competition law within the EU. Its role, and particularly, the powers granted to the Commission in deciding cases remain crucial to ensuring an effective enforcement of competition policy throughout the EU.

However, this paper also shows that, mostly from a procedural standpoint, convergence has not been fully achieved. In fact, a general application of the legal tools and powers introduced by Regulation 1/2003 is counter-balanced by sometimes divergent national procedures and regulations, resulting in potentially ambiguous scenarios.

---

[52]   See, *ex multis*, ICA decisions of July 29, 2004, No. 13457, case I559, *Mercato del calcestruzzo* and of April 26, 2006, No. 15392, case I603, *Gas tecnici industriali e medicali*.

[53]   See, *e.g.*, the judgment of the *TAR Lazio* No.1542/2008, *Mercato dello zolfo grezzo*.

[54]   See ICA decisions of June 14, 2006, No. 15604, case I641, *Rifornimenti aeroportuali*, and of April 26, 2006, No. 15392, case I603, *Gas tecnici industriali e medicali*.

[55]   See, *e.g.*, the judgment of the *TAR Lazio* No. 1733/2007, *Rifornimenti aeroportuali*; and the judgment of the *Consiglio di Stato* No. 1006/2008, *Gas tecnici*.

Divergences in procedures and competition law enforcement reduce legal certainty and often increase legal costs for undertakings, thus having a highly detrimental impact on business activities of companies operating within the EU. In light of this, the major challenge for the next ten years is the achievement of further convergence in antitrust enforcement. The active role of EU Member States – both alone and in the *forum* of the European Competition Network – will be decisive in this respect, especially in recognizing that a uniform application of EU and national competition law from both a substantive and procedural standpoint will contribute to the economic growth and stability of the Union.

PART III: INTERIM MEASURES PURSUANT TO ARTICLE 8 OF REGULATION 1/2003

■

Dr. Bernd Meyring[*]

I. Introduction

The Commission's power to adopt interim measures has been well established since *Camera Care*.[1] Regulation 1/2003[2] has further clarified the situation in Article 8. Interim measures require (i) a *prima facie* infringement and (ii) urgency. Whereas most of the relevant precedents are based on complaints or requests by third parties, such a request is not necessary. Article 8 even makes clear that interim measures do not primarily aim to protect individual positions or rights but competition as such from serious and irreparable damage.

Conceptually, there is no doubt that a competition authority needs powers to prevent anticompetitive conduct from causing irreparable harm while its investigation is pending. This is the basic reasoning behind *Camera Care*.[3] The collective or unilateral exercise of market power can lead to structural changes that have a lasting impact on markets. Even in the absence of such structural changes, some markets develop at a pace that may make regulatory intervention years after the conduct ineffective.[4]

---

[*] Partner at Linklaters LLP. The author thanks Mag. Lukas Solek for valuable input and comments on this paper.

[1] Case C-792/79 R, *Camera Care v. Commission*, [1980] ECR 119, §§ 17-19.

[2] Council Regulation (EC) No. 1/2003 of 16 December 2002 on the implementation of the rules on competition laid down in Articles 81 and 82 of the Treaty, *OJ* 2003, L 1, p. 1.

[3] Case C-792/79 R, *Camera Care v. Commission*, [1980] ECR 119, §§ 18-19.

[4] Of course, regulators should be prudent to intervene in quickly developing markets. An interventionist approach may well not be necessary or even counterproductive where market forces are eroding market power through innovation. But that does not mean that intervention in fast moving markets is *never* necessary and appropriate.

There is a stark contrast between the obvious conceptual need for the tool and the scarcity of its use. In fact, the Commission has adopted fewer than a dozen interim measures under the *Camera Care* doctrine and none under Regulation 1/2003. This contrast makes Article 8 an obvious candidate for further reflection when evaluating the functioning of Regulation 1/2003 and potential scope for reform. The Commission's evaluation after ten years of Regulation 1 does not discuss whether Article 8 needs reform. This paper therefore assesses the requirements and procedures for interim measures. It also discusses relevant examples and potential reasons for their small number. Against this background, it proposes conclusions on the instrument's suitability to prevent irreversible harm.

II. Requirements

Interim measures require (i) a prima facie infringement and (ii) urgency; (iii) they do not require a formal request by any company that would suffer harm in the absence of interim measures, but there are significant procedural requirements for the Commission to impose interim measures. A prima facie finding of infringement had already been required by *Camera Care*. The Commission only needs to show the appearance or probability of an infringement, which presupposes a less detailed analysis both as regards the underlying facts and the legal arguments.[5] Urgency requires *"the risk of serious and irreparable damage to competition"*. While Regulation 1/2003 adopted the *Camera Care* standard for the prima facie infringement, it opted for a much narrower definition of urgency and thereby reduced the potential scope for interim measures. The 2009 staff working paper[6] argues in this context that *"the purpose of Articles 81 and 82 EC is indeed to protect competition in the market"* and that the Commission's focus should be on protecting competition as such whereas national courts are better placed to protect the interests of individual companies.

Camera Care had allowed interim measures to prevent *"serious and irreparable damage to the party seeking their adoption, or which is intolerable for the public interest"*.[7] These measures therefore were meant to protect directly both individual and public goods. Article 8 of

---

[5]   Case T-184/01 R, *IMS Health Inc. v. Commission*, [2001] ECR 3193, § 68.
[6]   Commission Staff Working Paper accompanying the Report on the functioning of Regulation 1/2003 (SEC (2009) 574 final, 29.4.2009), § 111.
[7]   Case C-792/79 R, *Camera Care v. Commission*, [1980] ECR 119, § 19.

Regulation 1/2003 refers only to *"damage to competition"*. This indicates a limitation of the public interest. Further, Article 8 makes explicitly clear that interim measures are adopted ex officio, which is consistent with a tool that aims to protect the public rather than individual interests. Even a company that faces the threat of suffering irreparable harm does not have an individual right to interim measures. Just like enforcement action generally, interim measures therefore serve competition policy objectives and the Commission can decline to act if other authorities are better placed or if it makes the choice to use its resources differently, for example to investigate different conduct or to accelerate the decision on the merits in the same case. Harm to individual companies is only relevant to the extent that it coincides with or results from irreparable harm to competition as such.[8]

III. Procedure

Interestingly, the procedural framework for interim measures is essentially the same as applies to final decisions. It provides for a statement of objections and the right to be heard with regard to those objections, following access to the Commission's file. If the company requires an oral hearing, this hearing has to be held. Third parties that show sufficient interest and request to be heard may comment in writing and/or be admitted to take part in the hearing. Then, the Commission has to consult the Advisory Committee based on a draft decision. The final decision on interim measures is adopted by the full College followed by the summary publication. The addressee can file an action for annulment (and a request for interim measures) to the General Court.

Regulation 773/2004 does not provide for any accelerated or lighter procedures in the case of interim measures. This is in contrast with interim measures at the level of the European Courts, where interim measures can be adopted by the president and with procedural rules in the Member States, where interim measures can typically be adopted quickly, following procedural requirements that are lighter than for the decision on the merits.

---

[8] European Commission Antitrust Manual of Procedures, Internal DG Competition working document on procedures for the application of Articles 101 and 102 TFEU, March 2012 Module 17 "Interim Measures", §§ 5-9; see also § 15 that in contradiction to the wording of Article 8 of Regulation 1/2003 probably mistakenly provides that the existence of urgency is established even in cases which call for immediate action on the part of the Commission in order to avoid *"serious and irreparable damage"* to the party seeking the adoption of interim measures.

It is indeed somewhat surprising that Regulation 1/2003 provides for the possibility for an accelerated decision on interim measures but does not provide the tools that would enable the Commission to decide on interim measures far more quickly than it would decide on substance. The possibility to shorten the time to reply to a statement of objections in an interim measures case from four weeks to one (Article 17.2 of Regulation 773/2004) seems somewhat disappointing considering the total length of investigations under Regulation 1/2003.

In terms of substance, the company will not only have to be heard with regard to the prima facie infringement but also on the appropriateness and proportionality of the proposed interim measures.

Just like for decisions on substance, commitments can sometimes streamline proceedings and enable the Commission to act without going to a fully fledged infringement decision. There are several precedents before Regulation 1/2003 (*Napier Brown v. British Sugar,*[9] *Eurofix-Bauco v. Hilti*[10] and *Sea Container v. Stena Sealink*[11]), but the Commission has not used this tool since then. It has preferred to act swiftly on substance to restore competition, also in cases involving fast-moving markets such as *Microsoft,*[12] *E-Books*[13] and *IBM Maintenance Services.*[14]

The timeframe for interim measures under *Camera Care* varied considerably, between several weeks and the best part of a year.[15] However, this

---

[9] Case IV/30.178, *Napier Brown v. British Sugar, OJ* 1988, L 284, p. 41.
[10] Case IV/30.787 and 31.488, *Eurofix-Bauco v. Hilti, OJ* 1988, L 11, p. 3.
[11] Case IV/34.689, *Sea Container v. Stena Sealink, OJ* 1994, L 15, p. 8.
[12] *Microsoft,* Commission Press Release IP/09/1941 of 16 December 2009.
[13] Case COMP/AT.39.847, *E-Books, OJ* 2013, C 378, p. 25.
[14] Case COMP/C-3/39.692, *IBM Maintenance Services, OJ* 2012, C 18, p. 6.
[15] In *ECS v. AKZO* (Case IV/30.698, *ECS v. AKZO, OJ* 1983, L 252, p. 13) the procedure took several weeks. Following inspections at AKZO's premises in December 1982, the Commission opened the proceeding by its Decision of 8 June 1983. AKZO was given the opportunity to make known its views on the objections raised by the Commission pursuant to Article 19.1 Regulation 17/62. The Commission has also given the Advisory Committee on Restrictive Practices and Dominant Positions the opportunity to deliver an opinion. In *NDC Health v. IMS Health* (Case D3/38.044, *NDC Health v. IMS Health, OJ* 2002, L 59, p. 18) over six months elapsed between the lodging of a complaint accompanied by a request for interim measures and the adoption of the decision. Following several requests for information and meetings with pharmaceutical companies, the Commission initiated the proceeding against IMS Health by its Decision of 8 March 2001. On 9 March 2001 the Commission sent a Statement of Objections to IMS Health which had two weeks to comment in writing. IMS Health requested an oral hearing, which took place on 6 April 2001. IMS Health also provided the Commission with supplementary submissions which made it necessary to send out further requests for information and inform IMS Health of new findings. The last meeting between the Commission and IMS Health took place on 18 June 2001. The Decision was adopted on 3 July 2001.

was before the Commission was obliged by Regulation 1/2003 to essentially follow the procedure that applies to decisions on the merits. And it was also at a time of lighter scrutiny of competition decisions by the European Courts.

Limitation of Protected Interests

While the procedural burden on the Commission in interim measures cases has increased with Regulation 1/2003, the main pressure to adopt interim measures disappeared. Under *Camera Care*, interim measures were mainly triggered by complaints. They were a tool to preserve the position of market participants while a decision was pending. Of course, this had implications on the market structure and on competition more generally, but the trigger was typically a complainant's individual concerns. The complainant would support the Commission with facts and advocacy, in order to make sure that interim measures were adopted where necessary. The Commission had to provide reasons, not only if it adopted interim measures but also if it did not. Refusals could be challenged by complainants in Court.

Modernisation was a deliberate game changer in this respect. The basic objective was to push the application of the EU's competition rules to national authorities and courts. This would enable the Commission to define its priorities in line with its enforcement policy objectives. It could limit its enforcement activity to cases to which it was better suited than national authorities and judges – be it because a European precedent was needed or because practices concerned several Member States – and it was more efficient for the Commission to deal with them.[16]

This thinking also underpins Article 8 of Regulation 1/2003. The starting point is that national courts and regulators[17] are better placed to protect

---

[16] *La Serre/Lavedan*, Convergence and trends in the law and practice of interim measures ordered by competition authorities in Europe, *Concurrences* No. 2-2011, pp. 228-293.

[17] Several national legislations mention both damage to undertakings and to competition or public interest. This is for instance the case in Belgium where an interim measure can be adopted "in an urgent need to avoid situations likely to cause serious, imminent and irreparable damage to undertakings whose interests are affected by such practices or likely to harm the general economic interest" (Art. IV.64. § 1 of Book IV of the Code of Economic Law of 3 April 2013). In the UK, section 35 of the Competition Act 1988 refers to damage caused to a person, a category of persons or to the public interest. In France, it is sufficient to find an immediate and serious impact on the economy, the sector concerned, the consumers' interest or the plaintiff (Art L. 464-1 of the French Commercial Code). Indeed, the French Competition Authority has adopted more than 20 decisions imposing interim measures in the past 12 years (Bruno Lasserre, Economic Developments in European Competition Policy, Charles River Associates, Brussels, 10 December 2014).

individual interests than the Commission. They have tools to decide faster, are often closer to the facts and have processes that enable the balancing of adverse interests. By definition, interim measures are unlikely to affect the uniform application of substantive competition law in the EU. There is not the same need for the Commission to be involved as there may be in NCA decisions on substance.

This has significantly raised the bar for any interim measures cases by the Commission. Not only are there mechanisms in place that will often be better suited to deal with the interests at stake. Interim measures by the Commission also require that the Commission can establish the "*risk of serious and irreparable damage to the competition*", while "*acting on its own initiative*", in a process in which complainants will play a limited role.

The shift away from the protection of individual interests and complainants has removed the most significant trigger for interim measures in the past. Complainants were the instigators of most interim measures cases, since *Camera Care*.[18] They provided the Commission with information not only on the prima facie infringement but also on urgency and explained in detail the harm that they would suffer in the absence of interim measures. *Camera Care* had established that its business might be eliminated by insecurity of supply. ECS had established that the conditions offered by Akzo might force it into insolvency.[19] Brass Brand Instruments and others had shown the same risk in the absence of supply.[20] Similarly, interim measures in cases *IGR Stereo Television*,[21] *Amicon v. Fortia*,[22] *Napier Brown v. British Sugar*,[23] *Eurofix-Bauco v. Hilti*,[24] *Eco System v. Peugeot*,[25] *La Cinq v. European Broadcasting Union*,[26] *Sealink v. B&I*,[27] *Mars v. Langnese-Iglo and Schöller Lebensmittel*,[28] *Sea Container v. Stena Sealink*,[29] *Irish Continental Group v. CCI Morlaix*[30] and *NDC Health v.*

---

[18]   Case C-792/79 R, *Camera Care v. Commission*, [1980] ECR 119.
[19]   Case IV/30.698, *ECS v. AKZO*, OJ 1983, L 252, p. 13, §§ 33-34.
[20]   Case IV/32.279, *BBI v. Bossey & Hawkes*, OJ 1987, L 252, p. 13, §§ 22-23.
[21]   *IGR Stereo Television*, XI Commission Report on the Competition Policy (1981).
[22]   *Amicon v. Fortia*, XI Commission Report on the Competition Policy (1981).
[23]   Case IV/30.178, *Napier Brown v. British Sugar*, OJ 1988, L 284, p. 41.
[24]   Case IV/30.787 and 31.488, *Eurofix-Bauco v. Hilti*, OJ 1988, L 11, p. 3.
[25]   Case IV/33.157, *Eco System v. Peugeot*, Commission Press Release IP/90/233 of 27 March 1990.
[26]   Commission decision is not published; see to this end Case T-44/90, *La Cinq*, [1992] ECR 1.
[27]   Case IV/34.174, *Sealink v. B&I*, Commission Press Release IP/92/478 of 11 June 1992.
[28]   Case T-24/92 R and T-28/92 R, *Langnese-Iglo and Schöller Lebensmittel*, [1992] ECR, p. II-1839.
[29]   Case IV/34.689, *Sea Container v. Stena Sealink*, OJ 1994, L 15, p. 8.
[30]   Case IV/35.388, *Irish Continental Group v. CCI Morlaix*, IP/05/16 of 16 May 1995.

IMS Health[31] were adopted or considered following the application lodged by competitors of alleged infringers of Articles 101 and 102 TFEU. In all these cases, interim measures were adopted in order to avoid serious and irreparable damage to the applicants. Any damage to competition as such was only indirectly relevant and did not establish the urgency needed for interim measures.[32]

Ford is one of the few cases of interim measures on the Commission's initiative.[33] It aimed to protect parallel imports by a large number of car dealers in several countries without establishing that these companies would leave the market if they were to await the decision on the merits. The Commission's reasoning in that case is comparable to what Regulation 1/2003 requires. However, the ECJ annulled the Ford decision on procedural grounds and did not take a view on urgency.[34]

IV. Candidate cases for interim measures

The Commission referred to the risk of serious and irreparable damage to competition in some of the cases prior to Regulation 1/2003. Most concerned alleged exclusionary abuses of (alleged) dominant positions.[35] Where one undertaking dominates a market, the exclusion of an existing or potential competitor may affect the market structure in a lasting way. If entry becomes less likely or if there is the risk of a market exit, interim measures may well be appropriate in order to prevent irreparable changes to the market structure. For example, a refusal to supply may well not only delay but could also prevent market entry. In *BBI v. Bossey & Hawkes*,[36] Bossey & Hawkes refused to supply the complainants with instruments, spare parts and other materials. In *NDC Health v. IMS Health*[37] IMS Health refused to license its technology to manage data on sales in the pharmaceutical sector, the so-called "1860 Brick Structure" to its competitors. In

---

[31] Case D3/38.044, *NDC Health v. IMS Health*, OJ 2002, L 59, p. 18.

[32] See to this end in particular Case D3/38.044, *NDC Health v. IMS Health*, OJ 2002, L 59, p. 18.

[33] Case IV/30.696, *Distribution System of Ford Werke AG*, OJ 1982, L 256, p. 20.

[34] Case 228 and 229/82 R, *Ford Werke AG*, [1984] ECR 1129.

[35] There have so far been three cases where the Commission considered the risk of damage to competition. These cases concerned an alleged refusal to supply and predatory pricing; Case IV/30.698, *ECS v. AKZO*, OJ 1983, L 252, p. 13; Case IV/32.279, *BBI v. Bossey & Hawkes*, OJ 1987, L 252, p. 13; Case D3/38.044, *NDC Health v. IMS Health*, OJ 2002, L 59, p. 18.

[36] Case IV/32.279, *BBI v. Bossey & Hawkes*, OJ 1987, L 252, p. 13.

[37] Case D3/38.044, *NDC Health v. IMS Health*, OJ 2002, L 59, p. 18.

one isolated case, *ECS v. AKZO*[38] AKZO UK applied predatory prices with the aim of excluding the complainant as a competitor.

The risk to competition in most of these cases is that it results in potential harm to one or several specific undertakings. These acted as complainants before Regulation 1/2003 entered into force. In a post-modernisation world, these undertakings can, and arguably should, defend their interests in national courts. These national courts can find infringements and adopt interim measures to protect the undertakings. If they do, this should also deal with the risk for competition as such. While the Commission *could* still rule in these cases, it is far less likely to do so because national courts will often be better placed to deal with the situations. Where the Commission has already spent significant time and resources, if may be better placed than a national judge who had no prior involvement. However, even in such cases, the procedural requirements for interim measures at the EU level may mean that the national judge is better equipped.

Before Regulation 1/2003, the Commission considered the urgency test to be met where a decision on the merits would have come too late to prevent an irreversible change of the market structure. The risk of an irreversible market exit justified interim measures in cases like *ECS v. AKZO*,[39] *BBI v. Bossey & Hawkes*[40] and *NDC Health v. IMS Health*.[41] This necessarily involves an assessment of how markets would likely develop in the absence of interim measures at EU level. Where national court systems provide effective systems for relief and the relevant market players are likely to use them, the Commission may well conclude that interim measures at EU level are not necessary.

V. Conclusion

The Commission investigated 122 cases between 1 May 2004 and 31 December 2013,[42] without imposing any interim measures. However, this is not necessarily an indication that there is no longer any need for interim measures. Post-modernisation competition law enforcement certainly relies increasingly on national authorities and courts and these will often

---

[38] Case IV/30.698, *ECS v. AKZO*, OJ 1983, L 252, p. 13.
[39] Case IV/30.698, *ECS v. AKZO*, OJ 1983, L 252, p. 13.
[40] Case IV/32.279, *BBI v. Bossey & Hawkes*, OJ 1987, L 252, p. 13.
[41] Case D3/38.044, *NDC Health v. IMS Health*, OJ 2002, L 59, p. 18.
[42] Communication from the Commission, Ten Years of Antitrust Enforcement under Regulation 1/2003: Achievements and Future Perspectives (COM (2014) 453, 9.7.2014), § 8.

be better placed to deal with requests for interim measures. However, there is no justification to conclude that interim measures in a Commission case can never be appropriate. The Commission's staff is therefore right to consider that a mechanism for interim measures should be maintained.[43]

However, the procedural requirements for interim measures do merit further reflection. Is it really appropriate for the Commission to go through essentially the same procedural requirements as for final decisions? These procedural requirements are ill-suited to deal with situations of urgency, and competition law could be better enforced with more flexible procedures. The absence of interim measures for significant time under a more appropriate procedural framework would likely be a stronger indicator than the lack of precedents under Regulation 1/2003.

30 March 2015

---

[43] Commission Staff Working Document SWD (2014) 230, Ten Years of Antitrust Enforcement under Regulation 1/2003 (SWD (2014) 230/2, 9.7.2014).

PART IV: AN ECONOMIC PERSPECTIVE ON INDEPENDENT COMPETITION ENFORCEMENT

■

ALEXIS WALCKIERS[*], BENOÎT CRUTZEN[**] AND NICOLAS SAHUGUET[***]

I. Introduction

The manner in which investigations of alleged infringements are managed by competition authorities varies significantly across the world. While everyone would agree that the institutional design of competition authorities is crucial to ensure that competition law is enforced effectively, from a normative perspective, very little is known on how competition authorities should be organized.[1] How can effectivity (or independence) be measured in terms of different objectives such as deterrence of wrong-doing, right of defense, budget-saving, regulatory coherence or accountability? What are the relative merits of these objectives? In how far are they mutually exclusive?

An often discussed aspect of institutional design relates to the independence of competition authorities, which is sometimes viewed as indispensable. Some authors even suggest that effectiveness derives to some extent from independence:[2]

---

[*]   Belgian Competition Authority & Ecares – Université libre de Bruxelles.
[**] Erasmus Universiteit Rotterdam.
[***] HEC Montréal.
[1]   An increasing number of papers discuss institutional settings of competition authorities. See eg. D. CRANE, "The Institutional Structure of Antitrust Enforcement", Oxford, UK, Oxford University Press, 2011; D. A. HYMAN and W. E. KOVACIC, "Competition Agency Design: What's on the Menu?", *GWU Legal Studies Research Paper*, No. 2012-135; D. A. HYMAN. and W. E. KOVACIC, "Competition Agencies with Complex Policy Portfolios: Divide or Conquer?", *Illinois Program in Law, Behavior and Social Science Paper*, No. LE12-14, 2013; W. P. J. WILS, "Discretion and Prioritisation in Public Antitrust Enforcement, in Particular EU Antitrust Enforcement", *World Competition*, 34(3), 2011, pp. 353-382.
[2]   A. OTTOW, *Market & competition authorities: good agency principle*, Oxford, UK, Oxford University Press, 2015, p. 73.

> *"The independence principle encompasses the subvalues of objectivity, impartiality, integrity, expertise, and professionalism. These subvalues together adhere to the concept of overall independence and ensure that the independent agency can do its work effectively and independently. This principle therefore overlaps to some extent with the principle of effectiveness".*

Yet, not all competition authorities are structurally independent from elected politicians, and the manner in which independent decision-making is ensured differs widely:[3]

> *"It is generally agreed that competition agencies should be "independent" – i.e., that their actions should be based on the facts and the law and not political considerations. However, there is far less agreement to just how that should be accomplished as an organizational matter, and there is a multiplicity of organizational formats for competition agencies".*

Competition authorities have often developed over time to balance different objectives, which are unlikely to be weighted similarly across countries and across time. Furthermore, regulatory coherence requires that the design of the competition authority fits in the broader legal environment of the country and, as a result, what works well in one jurisdiction may not work as well in another.

This article reviews various economic arguments in favour of independent competition investigations, while highlighting a number of constraints deriving from independence. Focusing mainly on independence vis-à-vis elected politicians and on the separation of the functions of investigation and decision, we will in particular address three sets of questions:

– Who can influence decision-making, and from which interventions should decision-makers be protected?

– What are the main economic arguments to ensure that elected politicians cannot influence decisions of competition authorities?

– Why should those in charge of decision-making be independent of those in charge of investigations?

---

[3] International Competition Network Competition Policy Implementation Working Group (2009), "Seminar on competition agency effectiveness – Summary report", p. 27.

II. *Whom* should authorities gain *independence from?*

In essence, independence ensures that parties are treated in fair and impartial manner by the competition authority. But independence can be interpreted in different manners, depending on who has an incentive to bias decision-making, and how decision-makers can be protected against their influence?

Most competition practitioners focus on independence vis-à-vis elected politicians.[4] More precisely, the issue at stake is whether and in how far elected politicians can exert an influence on investigators or decision-makers to ensure that actions in a specific case diverge from the facts and the law towards their opinions or political considerations. In an article on an investigation on an alleged abuse of dominant position by Google, The Economist reports pressures by the European Parliament on the Commissioner in charge of Competition, and alludes that competitors may be trying to exert influence on elected politicians in charge of making the decision:

> "The European Parliament's Googlephobia looks a mask for two concerns, one worthier than the other. The lamentable one, which American politicians pointed out this week, is a desire to protect European companies. Among the loudest voices lobbying against Google are Axel Springer and Hubert Burda Media, two German media giants. Instead of attacking successful American companies, Europe's leaders should ask themselves why their continent has not produced a Google or a Facebook".[5]

Depending on the institutional setting, one can be concerned that elected politicians can influence the decision to open an investigation, the decision (not) to pursue an investigation, or the final decision.

In practice, politicians can seek to exert influence on decision making bodies of competition authorities through a wide variety of mechanisms, especially when they have the power to influence deciders' careers, or when their approval is required to allocate resources to the competition authority. Most obviously, those in charge of decision making may be concerned about their current and future careers; such career concerns can

---

4   See eg. OECD (2003), "OECD Global Forum on Competition: the objectives of competition law and policy" and International Competition Network Competition Policy Implementation Working Group (2009), "Seminar on competition agency effectiveness – Summary report".

5   *The Economist* (2014), "Should digital monopolies be broken up?", 27 November 2014.

be leveraged by politicians to induce their favoured decision. But, there are a wide variety of other, perhaps more subtle, manners for politicians to bias authorities' decisions, including incentives related to the budget of the authority.

But, next to the ability of elected politicians to influence decision-making, independence derives from a range of other factors. For instance, independence requires that parties are treated fairly, and that those in charge of investigating a case cannot influence the decision body, and vice-versa.

Issues surrounding the combination of the power to prosecute and take the final decision get a lot of attention in Europe. Although Courts[6] have never required that the European Commission separates its investigation teams, from those making the decision, it has in the past been subject to some criticism for not doing so. In 2005, the OECD underlined that "The Commission's integrated enforcement process, though efficient, has inherent weaknesses. Combining the functions of investigation and decision in a single institution can save costs but can also dampen internal critique".[7] This will be discussed in section IV.

Finally, an unbiased judiciary system usually relies on hearings, where the parties have the right to be heard by those in charge of taking the decision. This is not always the case in monist competition authorities, where parties are sometimes only heard by the team of the competition authority in charge of the investigation, but do not meet the final decision-makers in a formal hearing.

III. Arguments in favour of independent competition authorities

While for some practitioners the need for an independent competition authority appears evident, the type of argument invoked to justify independence differs widely. This section lists a range of reasons often referred to, which we have grouped into four categories: human rights, political economy, growth, and institutional design.

---

[6] See eg. D. SLATER, S. THOMAS and D. WAELBROECK, "Competition law proceedings before the European Commission and the right to a fair trial: no need for reform?", *The Global Competition Law Centre Working Papers Series*, Working Paper 04/08, 2004.

[7] OECD (2005), "Country studies: European Commission – Peer Review of Competition Law and Policy", p. 62.

A. Human right to an impartial tribunal

Article 10 of the Universal declaration of human rights and Article 6 of the European Convention on Human Rights (ECHR) provide that *"Everyone is entitled [...] to a fair and public hearing by an independent and impartial tribunal in the determination of [...] any criminal charge against him"*. The European Court of Human Rights has ruled that criminal character of an offence does not only depend on the nature of the offence. The criminal character of an offence within the meaning of Article 6 ECHR also depends on the nature and the degree of severity of the penalty. Competition investigations could therefore fall under the scope of Article 6 ECHR, to the extent that the fines imposed by competition authorities are *"very substantial"*.[8]

It is beyond the scope of this article to discuss whether and in how far the institutional setting of competition authorities should be modified to satisfy the requirements of Article 6 ECHR, but this is an argument that is put forward by a number of authors, such as Slater, Thomas and Waelbroek (2005).[9]

Given the rapid "criminalisation" of competition law proceedings, sanctions could in principle be imposed at first instance by an independent and impartial tribunal fulfilling all the conditions of Article 6 ECHR

B. Institutions and growth theory

Economists have since long investigated the causes of economic growth. Next to determinants such as physical or human capital, research and development or international trade, a number of economists have studied the role of sound institutions.

While it seems intuitive that sound institutions foster economic development, and while the most successful countries enjoy the benefits of efficient political institutions, it is more difficult to identify the mechanisms by which these institutions cause economic growth. In particular, while economic wealth is associated to sound institutions, it is unclear whether institutions foster wealth, or whether wealthy societies choose sound institutions.

---

[8] Judgement of the European Court of Human Rights of 8 June 1976 in *Engel and others v. the Netherlands and Judgment of the European Court of Human Rights* of November 23, 2006 in *Jussila v. Finland.*

[9] SLATER *et al.* (2004), *op. cit.*

Glaeser *et al.* (2004)[10] critically review the economic literature on institutions and growth.[11] They conclude that most studies on the subject cannot be used to identify the causal link (they "are conceptually unsuitable for that purpose"). The authors also highlight the role of human capital in fostering economic growth: some countries have shown that it is possible to accumulate human and physical capital to grow out of poverty under dictatorship; once these countries are richer, they can improve their political institutions.

Sound institutions appear to be particularly important for growth in already developed economies. Aghion, Alesina and Trebbi (2008)[12] highlight that the weak aggregate effect of democracy and institutions on growth is consistent with an effect that is different across sectors of the economy. According to the evidence the authors provide, political rights are key in more advanced sectors, while they matter less in less technological sectors, where the protection of vested interests is less problematic. While Acemoglu *et al.* (2014)[13] find that democracy also enhances growth in less developed countries, their results confirm that the effect of democracy on growth is most significant in countries where a larger proportion of the population has attended secondary school.

C. Institutional design: long term commitment

Another set of advantages of independent competition authorities relate to the institutional design of the organization, including the ability to attract qualified experts, the ability to react smoothly to changes, and the aptitude to credibly commit. Commitment is at the heart of a number of economic papers written in the 1980s and 1990s after Nobel Prize winners, Finn Kydland and Edward Prescott first highlighted how welfare is lowered by private decisions influenced by the inability of governments to make long-term commitments.[14]

---

[10] E. L. GLAESER, R. LA PORTA, F. LOPEZ-DE-SILANES and A. SHLEIFER, "Do Institutions Cause Growth?", *NBER Working Paper*, 2004, No. 10568.

[11] See also D. ACEMOGLU and J. ROBINSON, "The role of institutions in *growth* and *developmen*", *Working Paper*, 2008, No. 10, *Commission* for *Growth* and Development, The World Bank, Washington DC.

[12] P. AGHION, A. ALESINA and F. TREBBI, "Democracy, Technology, and Growth", in E. HELPMAN (ed.), *Institutions and Economic Performance*, Cambridge, Harvard University Press, 2008.

[13] D. ACEMOGLU, S. NAIDU, P. RESTREPO and J. A. ROBINSON, "Democracy Does Cause Growth", *NBER Working Paper*, 2014, No. 20004.

[14] The Royal Swedish Academy of Sciences (2004), "Finn Kydland and Edward Prescott's Contribution to Dynamic Macroeconomics: The Time Consistency of Economic Policy and the Driving Forces Behind Business Cycles," Advanced information on the Bank of Sweden

According to this literature, individuals in charge of monetary policy ought to be independent bureaucrats appointed to take care of long term economic growth, while elected politicians may be influenced by their (short-term) political objectives. Politicians might therefore implement policies that bring desirable outcomes in the short term (high economic growth and low unemployment), while undermining the economy's longer term potential.[15]

Some authors have drawn a parallel between the need for independent central banks and for independent competition authorities. Yet, as discussed by Vickers (2010)[16] competition authorities and central banks operate in different contexts. Vickers (2010) focusses in particular on the scope of their work, paraphrasing Isaiah Berlin's essay on Tolstoy: *The fox knows many things but the hedgehog knows one big thing.* Central banks concentrate on a single objective (low inflation), while competition authorities, like foxes, juggle with different tasks (merger control, abuses and cartels) across sectors. More broadly, the paper highlights a number of differences, including the exclusivity of the central bank in setting the interest rate and the one-off nature of decisions in competition investigations, while central banks revise their decisions periodically:

> *"The independent competition authority works in a system of law, making decisions, sometimes with long-lasting effects, about a variety of business practices in diverse markets, often on the basis of confidential information, under multi-faceted competition law, the meaning of which evolves and is not always clear, which others can also seek to apply, and subject to well-resourced challenges from interested parties, especially in court, where ultimate power lies with independent judiciary".*[17]

But despite these differences, Vickers (2010) concludes that competition authorities and central banks should be independent, to ensure that their decisions are only based on the long-run objectives of price stability and well-functioning markets:

Prize in Economic Sciences in Memory of Alfred Nobel, 11 October 2004, and F. KYDLAND and E. PRESCOTT, "Rules rather than discretion: The inconsistency of optimal plans," *Journal of Political Economy*, 1977, No. 85, pp. 473-490.

[15] See eg. R. BARRO and D. GORDON, "A positive theory of monetary policy in a natural-rate model", *Journal of Political Economy*, 1983, 91: 589-610; S. FISCHER, "Dynamic Inconsistency, Co-operation, and the Benevolent Dissembling Government", *Journal of Economic Dynamics and Control*, 1980, (1): 93-107; and T. PERSSON. and G. TABELLINI, "Designing Institutions for Monetary Stability", Carnegie-Rochester Conference Series on Public Policy, 1983, 39 (December): 53-8.

[16] J. VICKERS, "Central banks and competition authorities: institutional comparisons and new concerns", *BIS working paper* No. 331, 2010, Bank for International Settlements.

[17] *Ibid.*, p. 20.

"In sum, the prospects for the independence of monetary and competition (eg merger) policies post-crisis may depend above all on the answers to two questions. Are sound money and free markets still (appreciated as being) fundamental to long-run prosperity? Are there other important objectives that monetary and competition policies can usefully pursue in addition to price stability and markets free from threats to the competitive process? My answers, in short, would be yes and no respectively". [18]

D. Political economy: delegating technical tasks to non-elected bureaucrats

The independence of competition authorities vis-à-vis politicians can also be discussed on the basis of the political economy (or the public choice) literature. This literature seeks to compare the relative advantages of elected politicians and bureaucrats, and to identify under which conditions elected politicians should be preferred to bureaucrats:

- Elections allow the public to discipline officials, but they can induce politicians to "yield to public opinion and put too little weight on minority welfare" (Maskin and Tirole, 2004). [19] Coate and Besley (2000) show through a theoretical and an empirical study that elected officials tend to favour pro-consumers policies. [20]

- It is more efficient to opt for non-elected bureaucrats when: 1) the tasks to be performed require technical abilities (Alesina and Tabellini, 2007, and Maskin and Tirole, 2004); 2) the preferences of the public are known (Alesina and Tabellini, 2008); 3) the electorate is poorly informed about performance of officials (Maskin and Tirole, 2004); and 4) small but powerful vested interests care about the outcome (Alesina and Tabellini, 2007). [21] In the light of these papers, competition policy is best left to bureaucrats because it is a technical matter, that is difficult to explain to the wider public, and it is confronted to concentrated

---

[18] *Ibid.*, p. 31.

[19] E. MASKIN and J. TIROLE, "The Politician and the Judge: Accountability in Government", *American Economic Review*, 2004, 94(4): 1034-1054.

[20] COATE and BESLEY, "Elected versus Appointed Regulators: Theory and Evidence", *NBER Working Paper*, 2000, No. 7579.

[21] A. ALESINA and G. TABELLINI, "Bureaucrats or Politicians? Part I: A Single Policy Task", *American Economic Review*, 2007, 97(1): 169-179. A. Alesina and G. TABELLINI, "Bureaucrats or politicians? Part II: Multiple policy tasks", *Journal of Public Economics*, 2008, 92(3-4): 426-447; and A. MASKIN and J. TIROLE, "The Politician and the Judge: Accountability in Government", *American Economic Review*, 2004, 94(4): 1034-1054.

vested interests, but input or closer control of politicians is valuable, because it is complex to identify the preferences of the public, especially concerning priorities setting.

– But, the decision to delegate tasks is itself a political decision. Elected politicians who act to their own benefit (for example with a view to being reelected) may not be willing to delegate the appropriate policy tasks: they are happy to delegate risky policies "to shift risk (and blame) on bureaucracies", while retaining redistributive policies (Alesina and Tabellini, 2005).[22]

In summary, depending on their political background or on the region in which they want to be reelected, politicians in charge of competition policy could be biased in favour of (or against) a company or a sector. Although it is difficult to establish whether such claims are substantiated, there have been a number of press reports on EU commissioners being more receptive to arguments put forward by European companies (and even sometimes from their home country).[23]

IV. Separating the investigation and adjudicative functions

Article 10 of the Universal declaration of human rights and Article 6 of the European Convention on Human Rights (ECHR) require that those who incur a criminal penalty are heard by an independent tribunal. We will not return to the discussions of section 3.1 on the criminal nature of competition sanctions – and understand that the current arrangements with the possibility to appeal the decisions in front of the courts are sufficient from a human rights perspective – but we will discuss another aspect of independent decision-making: the separation of the investigative and adjudicative functions.

Functional separation is a much debated subject amongst competition practitioners. In Europe, a minority of authorities strictly separate both functions. In 2012, the European Competition Network[24] reported

---

[22] A. ALESINA and G. TABELLINI, "Why Do Politicians Delegate?", *NBER Working Paper*, 2005, No. 11531.

[23] In his last speech at AmCham EU, Vice-President Almunia denied that his actions were politically motivated: "This is why I can assure you that my request to Google to improve some aspects of its previous proposals is not due to any political pressure or to any bias related to its US origin. In fact, the main arguments I took into account as I asked for improved commitments were also provided by some US complainants".

[24] European Competition Network (2012), "Decision-Making Powers Report", Working Group Cooperation issues and due process, 31 October 2012.

that Belgium was the only European country that had chosen for a dual administrative system (the Belgian competition Authority was since then reformed in 2013, to a monist authority, with some separation of both functions within the authority). At the time, six countries had opted for judicial model in which investigations are carried out by the competition authority that brings the case before a court (where the decision making power lies). The bulk of European competition authorities, including the European Commission, are organized as monist administrative institutions that carry out the investigation and decide. There are different degrees of separation of the investigative and decision functions within these authorities. In the United States, the Department of Justice follows the judicial model, while the Federal Trade Commission carries out the investigation, and has some enforcement powers.[25]

The coexistence of different models has drawn a lot of attention on the pros and cons of these models. The main advantage of functional separation lies in the reduction of over-enforcement, but it is viewed as less resource efficient, and can lead to under-enforcement. Hyman and Kovacic (2014)[26] summarize the main tradeoff as follows:

> "The decision to unbundle or integrate involves tradeoffs between decision-making speed and expertise v. quality control and legitimacy. Tighter integration can accelerate investigation and resolution, by placing the key tasks in the hands of a body with specialized expertise. At the same time, integration can create difficulties with quality control problems, and also undermines procedural fairness".

We now describe these arguments in more details. The main advantage of separating the investigative and decisive functions is to better protect the rights of defense and thereby reduce the number of decisions in which the authority has wrongly sanctioned an innocent individual or company (false positives). Based on the behavioural economics literature,[27] Wils (2004)[28]

---

[25] For a detailed description of the enforcement powers of the FTC, see eg. https://www.ftc.gov/about-ftc/what-we-do/enforcement-authority.

[26] W. E. KOVACIC and D. A. HYMAN, "Competition Agency Design: What's on the Menu?", *GWU Legal Studies Research Paper*, 2012, No. 2012-135.

[27] See eg., The Royal Swedish Academy of Sciences (2002), "Foundations of Behavioral and experimental Ecnomics: Daniel Kahneman and Vernon Smith", Advanced information on the Bank of Sweden Prize in Economic Sciences in Memory of Alfred Nobel, 17 December 2002, M. RABIN, "Psychology and economics", *Journal of economic literature*, 1998, 36(1): 11-46.

[28] W. P. J. WILS, "The Combination of the Investigative and Prosecutorial Function and the Adjudicative Function in EC Antitrust Enforcement: A Legal and Economic Analysis", *World Competition*, 2004, 27(2): 201-224.

identifies 3 mechanisms by which the combination of both functions can lead to inaccurate decisions through the risk of prosecutorial bias:

- The confirmation bias leads humans to search for evidence that confirms their initial beliefs. As investigations are opened upon the belief that an antitrust violation is likely to be found,[29] the confirmation bias induces investigators to look for evidence of infringements. Within a hierarchical organization, investigators may be further encouraged to bias their results if they perceive that their hierarchy expects clear results.

- The hindsight bias and the desire to justify past efforts lead individuals to believe that what is apparent after an investigation should have been anticipated before the investigation was conducted. Decision-makers who have directly or indirectly contributed to the investigation – for example by deciding whether to open the investigation, or whether to pursue the investigation, or by taking part in discussions on how much resources should be allocated to the investigation – may be influenced by opinions they have expressed previously, or by the perception that they could have participated in wasting scarce resources by pursuing a useless investigation.

- The desire to show a high level of enforcement activity to observers, who themselves may find it difficult to assess the quality of the decisions taken and are therefore likely to focus on statistics of the number of decisions imposing fines, and the total amount of fines imposed.

However, separating the investigative and adjudicative functions also entails costs. Wils (2004) focuses on the higher administrative costs of separated entities, *"because [...] there will inevitably be some duplication in that the second person or group of persons has to acquire at least part of the knowledge of the case which the first person or group of persons will already have".* [30]

But, next to these direct costs, the separation of investigation and decision entails a range of indirect costs. In essence, these indirect costs arise from decision-making process under separation that does not necessarily improve accuracy. While Wils (2004)[31] does not envision this possibility, we summarize hereunder the leading arguments behind the idea that a

---

[29] *"[...] an investigation will normally be started only if the officials from DG Competition hold the initial belief that an antitrust violation is likely to be found"*, W. P. J. WILS (2004), *op. cit.*, p. 215.

[30] W. P. J. WILS (2004), *op. cit.*, p. 221.

[31] *Ibid.*

separated investigation team does not always lead to better investigations, a separated decision body does not necessarily improve decisions, and the separation itself requires coordination.

– Specialised teams – Hyman and Kovacic (2014)[32] argue that integrated authorities find it easier to involve specialized staff. Although the authors do not explicitly refer to economic input, it is an advantage of integrated authorities to be able to base their decisions on multidisciplinary and more specialized teams. Integrated authorities can specialize their teams because they have the size to do so (economies of scale and scope).

– Error by the decision-makers – Wils (2004)[33] believes that a specialized adjudicatory body always improves the quality of decisions, while this is not necessarily the case. It is possible that a correct interpretation of the law and the facts by the investigation arm of the authority is not followed by the decision arm. Such incorrect decisions can be caused by a lack of time or resources allocated to decisions, but can also be the consequence of behavioural biases such as social commitment, social pressure or reciprocity, which can induce deciders to wrongly accept some of the arguments developed by the defending parties.[34]

– Coordination failures – Coordination between the investigation and the decision arm can be deficient for various reasons. Most obviously, the investigation arm can spend time and resources to study issues that the decision arm does not consider relevant (which can be problematic under strict time constraints, as in merger review). Second, communication between the two arms typically follows strict procedures, which raises the probability that a procedural error occurs. In some cases, such procedural errors nullify the investigation. Finally, when both arms of the competition authority fail to coordinate their communication or methods, there is a risk that the predictability of law enforcement is undermined.

Unified competition authorities do not face these direct and indirect costs. They should therefore be traded off against the costs and benefits of a monolithic authority and taken into account when determining the budget of the competition authority. If this is not the case, competition law will

---

[32] W. E KOVACIC and D. A. HYMAN (2012), *op. cit.*

[33] W. P. J. WILS (2004), *op. cit.*

[34] See eg. D. DELLAVIGNA, "Psychology and Economics: Evidence from the Field", *Journal of Economic Literature*, 2009, 47(2): 315-372.

be under-enforced, which reduces the deterrent effect of the competition authority.

V. Conclusion

This short contribution discussed issues relating to the organization of a competition authority. We reviewed four categories of arguments in favor of independence of competition authorities vis-à-vis elected politicians. We also discussed the costs and benefits of functional separation. While most authors focus on the risk of over-enforcement resulting from a combination of investigation and decision, they typically overlook the risk of under enforcement and delay when these functions are not combined.

As a final note, we want to recall that, as much as we believe that researchers and practitioners should devote more attention to the analysis of the internal organization of competition authorities, what matters is whether and in how far competition authorities decide independently *in practice*. Most formal safeguards can be circumvented, while a number of competition authority that do not benefit from these safeguards are perceived as independent. Or in the words of Professor Giorgio Monti,

> *"It is well-established that some agencies may not appear independent when one considers the statute that establishes them but may develop significant degrees of independence over time. The best example is the Antitrust Division of the US Department of Justice: it is part of the executive branch and its head may be dismissed by the President; however in practice it normally exercises its powers largely independently of executive branch to which it belongs. Likewise the German Bundeskartellamt is under the supervision of the Minister of Economics but few doubt its independence".*[35]

---

[35] G. MONTI, (2014), "Independence, Interdependence and Legitimacy: The EU Commission, National Competition Authorities, and the European Competition Network," *EUI* Working Paper LAW 2014/01.

III

MODERNISATION 2.0 – OUTSTANDING ISSUES

PART V: ADVOCACY POWERS AND THE COMPETITION SCREENING OF NATIONAL LEGISLATION

■

SALVATORE REBECCHINI*

I. Introduction

The advocacy function of antitrust agencies, consisting in a broad range of activities aimed at fostering a "competition-friendly" environment, is expanding significantly; today it is considered, together with enforcement, the core business of an antitrust authority.

Overall, advocacy is considered complementary to the enforcement function. While the latter promotes allocative and productive efficiencies, by repressing anti-competitive behavior, advocacy aims at eliminating unnecessary restraints on market activities, thus fostering innovation and the creation of new enterprises (*i.e.*, dynamic efficiency). Complementarity works both ways: a good enforcement track record may give more weight and credibility to the advocacy activities of competition agencies, and the other way round, an advocacy initiative can facilitate an enforcement action, as the result of in-depth understanding of the functioning of the markets.

International organizations have come to recognize the importance of advocacy in promoting competition and liberalization measures to improve the performance of market based economies.

For instance, the International Competition Network (*ICN*) has a dedicated working group on advocacy which has developed many activities and a copious production of guidelines and recommendations. In December 2013, the Italian Competition Authority hosted the ICN workshop on "*Advocacy as a driver for change*".

---

* Commissioner, Italian Competition Authority. The usual disclaimer apply.

The OECD has produced the Competition Assessment Toolkit, first published in 2007 and then updated in 2010. The *"ex-ante"* competition assessment of law and regulation is becoming a widespread practice among OECD countries, as a part of the Regulatory Impact Assessment (RIA), after the publication of the OECD Recommendation on Competition Assessment (2009). Another international benchmark is also now available from ICN as well (2014 *Recommended Practices for Competition Impact Assessment*).

Last year the World Bank launched the Competition Advocacy Contest 2013 whose aim was to showcase the role of competition agencies in promoting competition. The project had a successful response, with the World Bank receiving more than 40 applications worldwide.

So, it is quite surprising that advocacy has been of so little concern to the ECN so far. This is at odds with the fact that all of its member agencies have been devoting much effort, on an individual basis, to conducting advocacy activities such as sector enquiries, often in industries of particular interest to European consumers.

II. Advocacy in ECN during the first ten years of Reg. 1/2003

Some advocacy activity has indeed taken place in the ECN framework.

First, it is worth mentioning the ECN work carried out in in the agriculture and food retail sector: in December 2012 the Heads of the European Competition Authorities adopted a *Resolution on the Reform of the Common Agricultural Policy* in response to the European Commission's proposal for a revised Regulation of the Common Agricultural Policy made in October 2011.

Some advocacy coordination is also performed through the interaction of case officers in the ten "working groups" on specific sectors (e.g., energy or food) or topics (e.g., fines, due process).

Finally, the bi-annual meetings of the heads of ECN agencies provide a mean for coordinated advocacy in the sense that they help to establish enforcement priorities of the network and, as a byproduct, they may foster common initiatives for opening markets by national competition authorities (NCA).

III. ECN as a network of advocates?

However, all of the above advocacy events are sporadic and insufficient, in my opinion. In an increasingly integrated Europe, where the threats to an open-competitive system have increased at the time of the severe economic downturn, the ECN should step up its role as a network of competition advocates. A more systematic approach is warranted in this respect, in order to enhance better coordination and experience sharing of the advocacy activities between the agencies of the network and provide stronger leverage to all members of the antitrust community across Europe.

Here are some proposals to strengthen the role of the ECN as a network for advocacy.

First, within the existing ECN Sectoral Working Groups, the advocacy activity should be more formal and systematic. Each group should envisage to hold a stock taking exercise of what advocacy is required and how it has been carried out in the respective sectors.

A second proposal is to establish an Advocacy Working Group in the ECN.

The first task of this Working Group would be to carry out a comparative survey of the advocacy powers and tools available to ECN agencies and how they have been used in practice: it is very important to gain a better understanding of each other's toolbox and experience.

The newly established ECN Working Group should represent an opportunity to share experiences, lesson learned and best practices in relation to:

4. Instruments to be available in the advocacy tool-box. Several tools can be useful for advocacy: market inquiries, formal opinions delivered to government entities, outreach activities with business and consumer associations, specialized events with stakeholders and academia.

5. Defining strategies: how to identify and select advocacy opportunities, what should be the most effective mix of advocacy tools; what is the appropriate mix of proactive vs. reactive initiatives.

6. Performing competition assessment of legislation.

7. Engaging with sectoral regulators.

8. Measuring the effectiveness of advocacy: how to evaluate if advocacy "worked" or not?, what the weight to be given to short *vs* long term objectives for advocacy.

The ECN Advocacy Working Group could also encourage members to improve coordination of advocacy initiatives at national level – especially market enquiries – to improve effectiveness and economize resources.

These coordination efforts may be advisable for advocacy initiatives concerning sectors not covered by EU legislation, such as professional services, distribution and retail.

One example of informal – and maybe inefficient – advocacy coordination can be found in the food sector. Since 2005, more than 10 agencies have completed market enquiries, leading to the emergence of a pattern of highly interesting common findings. Of course, national agencies took into account each other reports, and exchanged methodological issues, on a case-by-case basis as well as at ECN level. The Commission stepped in in the final phase to wrap up the results of the national enquiries. Notwithstanding the interesting outcome of the multiple enquiries, if coordination had taken place at an earlier stage, with plans to simultaneously launch an inquiry on the same topic and with the same criteria, a better overall picture could have been taken of the sector across the EU.

Also, an ECN Advocacy Working Group within ECN may be useful to support DG Comp when advocating changes or reforms at European level, in order to engage other Directorate General of the Commission or other European Institutions, responsible for policies and regulation.

The third and last proposal is more ambitious. A standardization of Advocacy instruments across the EU could be pursued through the reform of Reg. 1/2003. It could be envisaged that a standard toolkit of advocacy instruments should be adopted by ECN members and some common procedures could be established to enable EU-wide advocacy initiatives. This could help develop synergies across the Union to contrast anticompetitive initiatives that could develop in a plurality of member States and protect the single market.

IV. Advocacy toolbox of the Italian NCA

The set of powers and tools available to the Italian Competition Authority (ICA) is rather broad. Recently the ICA engaged in a monitoring exercise of its advocacy activity towards Government, legislators and central and local administrative bodies. This is the outcome, in the period from January 2013 to June 2014, according to the different instrument utilized:

- 34 opinions on existing legislation (art 21); success rate: 26%;[1]

---

[1] Success rate indicates the percentage of cases in which the recipient complied with the Authority's opinion.

- 74 opinions on draft legislation (art. 22), divided in:
  - ○ 22 opinions on request of central Public Administration (PA): success rate 73%;
  - ○ 12 opinions on request of local PA: success rate 50%;
  - ○ 21 opinions *ex officio*: success rate
    - 20% for opinions to a central PA;
    - 50% for opinions to a local PA;
  - ○ 19 opinions to the Presidency of Council of Ministers (PCM) in charge of reviewing the compatibility of the draft legislation proposed by the Regions with national legislation and Constitution principles: in 9 cases the Authority's opinion was used by the PCM to challenge the act before the Constitutional Court (success rate of 47%). In 5 out of 9 cases, the Constitutional Court confirmed the ICA's concerns (success rate of 55%);
- 26 opinions on administrative acts (Art. 21-*bis*), with the power of initiating court proceedings to repeal act in case of non-compliance; success rate of 77%.

Based on the Italian experience, it can be noted that:

- Advocacy is more effective on draft legislation than on existing laws. The process for amending or removing an existing law generally requires time and the political consensus built around the enacted legislation is more difficult to change given the vested interests that have been created.
- Advocacy on existing regulations is more effective when the opinion or recommendation of the competition agency has some enforcement power as in the case of Art. 21-*bis* of the Italian Antitrust Law.
- The possibility to advocate on secondary legislation is crucial to ensure success of liberalization measures. In the Italian institutional framework, legislative and regulatory powers in many important sectors are exclusive competence of regional and local authorities or, at the best, shared with the central government with unclear boundaries. In some cases (*i.e.* retail distribution), advocacy initiatives by ICA has prevented local authorities from watering down the liberalization measures established by the national legislator.

The Italian Competition Authority has also stepped up a pro-active strategy of advocacy, whereby a broad set of proposals are issued not only to react to the introduction of unduly restrictive measures, but also to stimulate the Government to liberalize and open market to competition.

The ICA, for instance, has taken a pro-active approach in the context of the Annual Law for Competition. According to this law, enacted in 2009, every year the Government is asked to present to Parliament a liberalization bill, taking into account the opinions and the recommendations delivered by the ICA over the years. To facilitate this task, on several occasions the Italian authority compiled a broad comprehensive report containing a menu of liberalization measures, covering different sectors, selected on the basis of ICA's evaluation of their potential impact on competition and growth.[2]

These comprehensive reports represent an opportunity for stimulating the debate on pro-competitive reforms. By addressing many different sectors, these proposals may be perceived as more equitable and help mobilize public opinion support for the reforms and counter the inevitable opposition of vested interests. Moreover, they allow the ICA to take stock of its opinions submitted over the years and monitor their implementation.

In these reports, the Italian Competition Authority has cited the ECN Recommendations of December 2013 as a rationale for change and to build support with the legislator. For instance, in its 2012 submission to the government, ICA made several proposals to ensure the effectiveness of the leniency program and therefore cartel detection, based on the position publicly taken by the Commission and the NCAs in relation to the role of private and public enforcement of competition law in the EU.

V. A more systematic approach to the monitoring of Authority's recommendations

Following up on the stock taking exercise, the ICA is exploring various initiatives to improve the effectiveness of its advocacy activities.

These initiatives include:

1. Improve the rate of response by the addressee:
   - Ask the addressee to provide a reply within a specific term;
   - Where no answer is provided, replicate the request.
2. Work closer with Courts:
   - Especially in the most important cases, the Authority could issue *ad adiuvandum* opinions in administrative proceedings related to antirust matters.

---

[2]   See, for instance, Authority's advocacy reports for the Annual Law for Competition (AS1137 in 2014, AS988 in 2013, AS901 in 2012) are available at: http://www.agcm.it/segnalazioni/legge-annuale.html.

3. Foster competition culture:
   - Carry out monitoring activities on a yearly basis;
   - Highlight through press release successful Advocacy initiatives;
   - Publish regularly outcome of monitoring activities;
   - Engage with professional categories, associations, and local authorities to present results of advocacy interventions at national and local level.

VI. Conclusions

The need to promote an open pro-competitive environment has become a crucial objective among the highly integrated economies of the EU, especially at the time in which growth and competitiveness are faltering. In this respect, an increasing role of the ECN with respect to the advocacy activity would be welcomed, particularly in order to foster common initiatives that would benefit the single market at large.

The Italian Competition Authority is provided with a rather broad set of advocacy instruments utilized to enhance and support pro-competitive initiatives both of a reactive and a pro-active nature. The experience gathered by Italy with this set of instruments constitutes a useful background for discussing the adoption of a common advocacy tool-kit at the EU level.

PART VI: THE FUTURE OF JUDICIAL REVIEW AT BOTH NATIONAL AND EU LEVELS

SANTIAGO SOLDEVILA FRAGOSO[*]

As a former judge at the General Court and, currently, a judge of the Audiencia Nacional in Madrid, I will start by explaining how I see the future of the General Court, the backlog of cases it faces and potential solutions. I will finish with the topic of the review by national courts of decisions by national competition authorities, stressing the paradox that exists in the belief of the highest level of protection of fundamental rights by national courts and yet, in some jurisdictions, competition law cases are decided without an oral hearing.

I. The future of the General Court

A. The General Court has a problem

The General Court (GC) is not able to deal within a reasonable timeframe with all the cases registered.[1]

The internal measures adopted in 2008, in an effort to increase the Court's productivity, have been certainly effective but not sufficient. By way of illustration, the number of new cases registered each year is larger than the number of final decisions taken.

The 2012 and 2013 statistics of the Court show that each judge deals with more than 25 cases per year as a judge rapporteur. It must also be taken into consideration that those judges have to study all the cases allocated to its chamber, composed of 3 or 5 members: that equates to about 80 cases per year. Furthermore, they contribute to the general assembly and different committees. Taking into account those additional obligations, one

---

[*] Judge at the General Court (2007/2013); Judge at the Audiencia Nacional, Madrid.
[1] In 2014, new cases were 912, completed cases were 814, and pending cases were 1423.

can conclude that it is necessary to take structural measures to solve this problem of delay in the adjudication of cases by the GC.

The Court of Justice (CJ) and the European Commission (EC) are attempting to address this point and on 28 March 2011 a proposal was made to increase the number of judges of the GC (12 posts).

On 3 September 2014, the EC invited the CJ to put forward new suggestions.

The final proposal of the CJ, dated 20 November 2014, is to increase the number of new judges to 28, one for each Member State, in three stages: The first stage to occur in 2015 (12 new judges), the second stage to occur in 2016 (7 new judges transferred to the GC from the Civil Service Tribunal (CST)), and the third stage to occur in 2019 with an increase of 9 new judges.

The creation of a specialized jurisdiction for matters of intellectual property rights (IPR) has been rejected.

Are the above proposals a proper solution? I am afraid not.

B. Two options, one solution

It is true that the Treaty foresees two different structural measures to cope with the rise of pending cases and the right of citizens to effective protection of the fundamental right to a judicial decision within a reasonable time:[2] the creation of specialized jurisdictions and the increase in the number of judges.[3]

A superficial analysis of the Treaty could support the idea that the choice between both propositions is just a political decision belonging to the CJ or the EC.

In my view, a systematic interpretation of the Treaty shows that each measure foresees dealing with a specific problem: when the rise in the number of cases concerns a specific subject, i.e. IPR, the only structural solution is the creation of a specialized jurisdiction in this field. On the contrary, when the rise in the number of cases is horizontal, the only solution is the increase of the number of judges of the GC.

This approach guarantees the efficacy of the Treaty because the creation of a specialized jurisdiction is only possible when an increase in the number cases relates to a specific matter.[4]

---

[2] Article 47 of the Charter of Fundamental Rights.
[3] Articles 254 and 257 of the Treaty on the Functioning of the European Union (TFEU).
[4] S. SOLDEVILA FRAGOSO, "La création de juridictions spécialisées: la réponse du Traité au traitement des contentieux de masses", Revue Europe, No. 2, February 2011.

C. The creation of a specialized jurisdiction: Analysis

1. Justification for its creation

a) The number of cases:

When the Civil Service Tribunal (CST) was created,[5] the number of civil service cases registered in the GC was 146 in 2004, 124 in 2003 and 112 in 2002. The number of cases registered in 2014 at the GC concerning IPR was 295 and a further sharp increase is foreseeable for 2015.

b) The subject:

IPR is a specific one, and it must be taken into account that the vast majority of IPR cases concerns the interpretation of Articles 7 and 8 of Council Regulation 207/2009 of 26 February 2009 on the Community trademark.[6]

c) The impact of Article 67 of the Rules of Procedure (RP) of the GC, and some existing case law, such as the judgment of the CJ of 16 July 2009, C-385/07, point 182, "Der Grüne Punkt":

– Article 55 RP states that the GC shall deal with the cases before it in the order in which the preparatory inquiries in them have been completed, and the jurisprudence quoted considers the complexity of the matter as a criterion in order to justify the delay in the resolution of cases;

– IPR cases can be complex, but give rise to specific and homogeneous questions, the majority of which have been set out already in existing jurisprudence, so there is no reason to justify a delay in this instance.

d) The problem:

According to those rules, IPR must be decided in a short time frame.

The consequence of undue delays is that the GC gets blocked up and is no longer able to resolve the other cases without an unreasonable delay. As a consequence, cases which involve the analysis of vast and complicated files, like competition law cases, are systematically delayed.

What is more, those complex cases concern not only private companies, but also the Member States, who have a legitimate interest in receiving swift judgments in order to use some enterprises as instruments of their economic and social policy.[7]

---

[5] Council Decision of 2 November 2004 establishing the European Union Civil Service Tribunal (2004/752/EC, Euratom).

[6] Opinion of AG Jacobs of 21 march 2002, C-50/00, *Union de pequeños agricultores*, pt 81.

[7] Judgment of the CJ of 20 April 2010, C-265/08, *Federutility*, pt 28.

e) IPR cases are of a private nature. Conflicts arise, normally, between two companies and the Member States are not involved.[8]

The above-listed circumstances make it easy to justify the creation and the development of a specialized jurisdiction for IPR.

2. Direct and positive impact for the General Court

a) Nearly 40% of the cases annually registered at the General Court would be transferred to this new specialized jurisdiction for IPR cases, once it is put in place.

b) The GC will be ready to focus its efforts on the most cumbersome cases, normally competition law cases.

c) The GC will keep its institutional position as an intermediate level in the European legal framework, as the Treaty provides.

3. The creation of a new specialized jurisdiction permits a more efficient and rational way in which to deal with IPR cases

a) New judges, selected among experts in this field, should be able to guarantee the quality of the judgments and provide a quicker answer to the pending cases.

b) There is a broad body of case law published since 1996 by the CJ and the GC, which can provide a basis for their decisions.

c) The small number of judges needed for this Court, about 9, permits the discussion of the cases in a plenary session. This technique guarantees the consistency of the jurisprudence.

d) Two "*ad hoc* judges" can be appointed for the stability of the Court in cases of vacancy for an exceptional reason, *i.e.* in case of serious disease.

e) The new jurisdiction can provisionally adopt, as the CST did, the Rules of Procedure of the GC, which have a specific chapter for IPR cases.

f) The positive experience of the CST confirms all these points.[9]

---

[8] T-526/09, *Paki logistics/OHMI*, involved, exceptionally, a Member State: the UK.
[9] See the comments and conclusions of the 5 th anniversary of the Civil Service Tribunal. www. Curia.europa.eu.

4. Impact for the Institution

a) The financial cost of a specialized jurisdiction is lower than the increase of the number of judges in the GC, for two reasons: firstly because only 9 judges, not 28, are needed, and secondly because judges in a specialized jurisdiction need a smaller amount of staff, just like the CST has. For example, judges of specialized jurisdictions have only one clerk and one secretary. Judges of the GC have three clerks and two secretaries.

b) The creation of a new specialized jurisdiction, with 9 new judges, may help the Member States with the negotiations for the appointment of the judges of the CST, which, at the moment, are at an impasse.

D. The increase of the number of judges: Analysis of the proposal made by the Court of Justice

1. The integration of 7 judges into the GC, coming from the CST, is controversial for the following reasons

a) There is no reason to change the nature, structure and functioning of the CST, given the positive evaluation of its progress thus far.

On the contrary, the integration of CST judges into the GC implies that the appeals against the GC's decisions should be decided by the CJ, thus increasing the number of pending cases.

This is contrary to the mandate of the Treaty, which clearly established three levels of jurisdictions. The Treaty provides that appeals to the judgments of the CST, which is a specialized jurisdiction, go to the GC, which is not organized in specialized chambers.

b) Judges coming from the CST, who are specialists in this field, cannot automatically be appointed as new judges of the GC. They must be put forward by their States and be approved by the Council and they then have to be examined by the Committee established by Article 255 of the TFEU. Although these judges have been selected for the CST according to their specific knowledge in civil service cases, Article 254 TFEU stipulates that in order to be appointed a judge of the GC, one must fulfill the requirements for appointment to high judicial office.

c) Accordingly, there is no guarantee that, for example, these 7 new judges are specialists in the area of civil service, despite the fact they have to replace judges of the CST.

d) The creation of a specialized chamber inside the GC to deal with those cases would have been the natural consequence of this proposal, but unfortunately, this is contrary to the provisions of the Treaty, because in the latter the word "specialization" is linked to the creation of a new jurisdiction.

e) The allocation of similar or connected cases to the same Chamber is a rational and efficient distribution of the work in the Court, absolutely compatible with the Treaty, but this is different from Court specialization, which requires a huge number of cases concerning a specific sector of the law, *i.e.*, civil service, intellectual property rights, State aid, competition law being decided by a specialized Court.

2. The appointment of 21 new extra judges creates problems

a) The effect of this measure is not instantaneous:

– When a new jurisdiction is created, there is an immediate transfer of cases from the GC to the new jurisdiction, however when new judges merely arrive at the GC, the stock of cases to be decided remains *in the GC*.

– The output of the addition of new judges only becomes apparent after one year, as that is the minimum time required in order to see through even the most simple of cases at the GC.

b) A large share of those 21 extra judges will be obliged to deal only with IPR cases, according to the reasons we explained in point 3.1, but judges of the GC, according to the provision of Article 254 TFUE, are not specialized judges.

c) Specialized chambers for IPR cases should not be created in the GC as this only increases the problem that we described in point 4.1.

3. The inconsistency of the proposed system

– The proposal of the CJ implies the creation of some specialized chambers and the appointment of some specialized judges for the GC. The correct functioning of these specialized chambers demands stability in their composition, so the rotation of the GC judges to different chambers is not sensible. Another factor contributing towards instability is the fact that the judges have a mandate lasting only 6 years and a new appointment is not a guarantee for any years beyond this.

– Nevertheless, these judges will have a general knowledge of European law, and they will most likely be interested in dealing with, not only civil service and IPR cases, but also with economically complex cases such as those relating to competition law, State aid, or antidumping.

– The practice of judges rotating is contrary to the efficacy of the new system proposed by the CJ.

– The question arises: are some Member States going to put forward judges who shall deal only with civil service and IPR cases, thereby renouncing influence on some of the most important economic cases, where big national companies and even Member States are involved?

4. The internal organization of the GC, specially the plenary meeting, becomes extremely complicated

When an organization has a large number of members, the level of participation and direct contact between them becomes very difficult and in the case of an international jurisdiction, this kind of contact is extremely important.

E. Why does the Court of Justice reject the creation of the specialized jurisdiction?

The proposal of the CJ in the reasoning document describes some arguments to reject the creation of a specialized jurisdiction in IPR. The majority of those arguments have been addressed in this document.

It is important to stress that the Treaty considers as normal the creation of new specialized jurisdictions when circumstances so require, therefore their creation is not an exception.

On the contrary, this should be the ordinary solution for the rise in the number of specific cases:

– In fact, the main concern of the CJ is that the development of this structure implies that appeals and preliminary rulings, concerning the specialized jurisdictions, are to be decided by the GC without the real control of the CJ.

That means that the GC becomes a multi-function body, so at the same time is a first instance jurisdiction, and a Constitutional and Supreme Court.

– This final outcome is not satisfactory for the CJ and in this respect it is necessary to give a satisfactory answer to those concerns of the CJ about the creation of specialized jurisdictions.

Therefore, it is necessary to find a mechanism by which the supremacy of the CJ is guaranteed.

F. The Court of Justice judgment of 19 September 2013, *Strack*, C-579/12 and its influence

The first paragraph of Article 256.2 of the TFEU provides that the GC acts as an appeal court reviewing decisions of the specialized Courts. The second paragraph of this article provides that the decisions of the GC may exceptionally be subject to review by the CJ, under the conditions and within the limits laid down by the Statute, where there is a serious risk of the unity or consistency of Union law being affected.

Despite the wording of Article 256.2, its application has until now been insufficient to achieve its aim because of the strict interpretation made by the CJ of the concept "serious risk for the unity or consistency of Union law".

The judgment in Strack offers a new and interesting approach:[10]

– The classical approach of the CJ was to refrain from judging the evolution of the jurisprudence of the chamber of appeal of the GC, and is described in the *Petrilli* judgment, C-17/2011, point 4, where the CJ said:

> "First, it is not for the Court of Justice, in the context of the review procedure, to rule on the merits of the General Court's development of its own case-law when acting in its appellate capacity. Second, the fact that the Court of Justice has not yet ruled on a point of law is, in itself, not sufficient to justify a review pursuant to Article 62 of the Statute of the Court of Justice of the European Union, in so far as it is now solely for the Civil Service Tribunal and the General Court of the European Union to develop the case-law in matters relating to the civil service, since the Court of Justice has jurisdiction only to prevent the decisions of the General Court affecting the unity or consistency of European Union law".

– In the *Strack* judgment the CJ changes its approach about the limits of its competence in reviewing cases and offers a new and more flexible

---

[10] An interesting analysis of this judgment: Éléonore von Bardeleben, "La procédure de réexamen, instrument d'une application prétorienne audacieuse des directives aux institutions européennes" (commentaire de l'arrêt CJUE, 19 septembre 2013, aff. C-579/12 RX-II, *Commission c/ Guido Strack*), *Revue trimestrielle de droit européen*, No. 1 (2014), pp. 111-132 n.

definition of the concept *"the unity and consistency of European Union law"*. Accordingly, the CJ overruled the judgment of the GC and decided that:

> *"The errors of law vitiating the judgment of 8 November 2012 [...] are such as to adversely affect the unity and consistency of European Union law. By dismissing, in its interpretation of the provisions of the Staff Regulations, the notion of the right of every worker to paid annual leave as a principle of the social law of the European Union now affirmed by Article 31(2) of the Charter and referred to, inter alia, in Article 7 of Directive 2003/88, as interpreted by the settled case-law of the Court of Justice, the General Court caused an adverse effect, in particular, on the unity of European Union law since a provision such as the above mentioned provision of the Charter, has the same legal value, pursuant to the first subparagraph of Article 6(1) TEU, as the provisions of the treaties and the Union legislature is required to observe it both when it adopts a measure such as the Staff Regulations on the basis of Article 336 TFEU and when it adopts other measures of European Union law under the legislative power invested in it under other provisions of the treaties and, moreover, in the Member States when they implement such measures. 'This new approach, more complete in the analysis of the substance of the cases, can guarantee the supremacy of the CJ in the areas of European law submitted to specialized jurisdictions'".*

G. Is the Review Procedure a kind of writ of certiorari and a potential solution for this problem?

It´s important to note that the Review Procedure by the CJ under Article 256.2 TFEU, like the writ of certiorari, is not an appeal, but a petition to the Supreme Court asking for a new judgment. It is clear that such a review is not a third instance.

It is important to stress the similarities between the Review Procedure and the writ of certiorari and the fact that since 1988, the writ of certiorari has been the ordinary option to accede to the Supreme Court of the USA and a very important tool for increasing its influence and power.

The main feature of the certiorari is the discretion granted to the Supreme Court to decide whether a decision of the Federal Court is to be reviewed and to indicate only those questions which it intends to review (excluding, of course, cases on the grounds of the correction of factual errors). The petition can be rejected without providing reasoning.[11]

This is exactly the scope that the Review Procedure is granted in Article 256 of the TFEU, Article 62 of the Statute of the CJ, and Articles 191 to 195 of the Rules of Procedure of the Court of Justice. It is true that Article 62 of the Statute of the CJ provides that only the First Advocate-General may propose that the CJ reviews a decision of the GC, but a discussion as to the modification of the Statute of the CJ in this respect should be initiated.

Finally, it is necessary to point out that, according to Article 256.2 of the TFEU, where the General Court considers that the case requires a decision of principle likely to affect the unity or consistency of Union law, it may refer the case to the Court of Justice for a ruling.[12]

The conclusion is obvious: the fact that the GC would be competent to settle some cases as if it was a Supreme or even a Constitutional Court, is not a challenge to the supremacy of the CJ and the new approach of the Review Procedure according to the Strack judgment confirms this fact.

H. The General Court as a *hidden specialized* jurisdiction for competition law cases?

The GC was created in 1989 as a specialized Court for civil service and competition law cases.

In 2005, according to the provisions of the Nice Treaty, the CST was created due to the increase in the number of cases in the civil service field, which was blocking the ordinary activity of the GC.

The particular features of competition law cases, where big companies and even the Member States are involved, and with different economic and judicial approaches, are such that all Member States involved must be represented in the Court.

Nevertheless, it will not be possible to justify a Court with 28 judges dealing only with competition law cases. For this reason, according to the purpose of the Nice and Lisbon Treaties, the GC has to deal not only

---

[11] M. Ahumada Ruiz, "Certiorari y criterios de selección de casos en última instancia: qué casos, cuántos casos" en la obra colectiva *La defensa de los derechos fundamentales: Tribunal Constitucional y Poder Judicial*, pp. 59-64, Centro de Estudios Políticos y Constitucionales, Madrid 2010.

[12] Free circulation of goods can be involved in preliminary rulings concerning IPR cases but the number of cases per year is not significant, so referring those cases to the CJ does not hamper the system. Vid, point 32 of the article quoted at footnote No. 3.

with competition law cases, but also with all other cases as set out in the Treaties. This fact is justified in the name of the court itself, "General Court", which demands a general knowledge in European law from its duly appointed judges.

However, given that the judicial review of competition law cases constitutes a prominent part of the activity of the GC, and that it was the main reason for which it was created, specialized cases in other fields should not hamper the principal activity of the GC.

It follows from the foregoing that in order to preserve the main and original activity of the GC, which involves big economic consequences concerning the core of the single market, when a sector of new specialized cases, such as IPR cases, increases in number and, as a result, congests the activity of the GC, a specialized jurisdiction should be created to guarantee the smooth running of the ordinary activity of the GC.

II. Judicial review at national level: some current problems

The comparison between the practice of both European and Spanish national jurisdictions reveals some paradoxical aspects.

A. Higher protection of fundamental rights at Spanish level

In the European culture and judiciary systems, the respect for fundamental rights is out of discussion. Nevertheless, the degree of protection is not the same in all the Member States and inside the EU.

Spanish jurisprudence concerning administrative cases, more specifically, administrative sanctions, is more protective for the defendant than the European case law concerning sanctions imposed under Articles 101 and 102 TFEU.

Despite this, Spanish judges, as all national judges of the EU, have to respect the decisions of the GC and the CJ when European law is involved. According to that, a double standard of protection is applied, even when the same fundamental right is invoked, depending on the European or national nature of the legislation.

A recent example of this statement is the CJ judgment of 18 June 2013, *Schenker*, C-681/11, point 36. This judgment decided that:

"If, in the general interest of uniform application of Articles 101 TFEU and 102 TFEU in the European Union, the Member States establish conditions relating to intention or negligence in the context of application of Article 5 of Regulation No. 1/2003, those conditions should be at least as stringent as the condition laid down in Article 23 of Regulation No. 1/2003 so as not to jeopardise the effectiveness of European Union law".

This doctrine reduces the margin of discretion of national judges in reviewing sanctions according to the national practice and displaces national jurisprudence if it is less severe than the European one. This is, in fact, the natural consequence of the primacy of the European law (CJ judgment of 6 March 2014, *Siragussa*, C-206/2013, pt 32).

B. The real absence of hearings at the Spanish level

Nevertheless, after my personal experience as a Judge of the GC, I can conclude that hearings are the most important procedural guarantee in review cases.

Hearings permit the direct confrontation of all arguments, the detailed analysis by judges of all the evidence and the real collegiality of the decision.

Although Spanish law foresees, as an option, the oral phase of the procedure, in practice judges never concede it.

The main reason is related to the number of cases that each judge is obliged to settle per year, about 150 as judge rapporteur in chambers of five members.

Those cases are normally about big issues. For instance, the Audiencia Nacional is the competent body to review the administrative activity of the members of the Government.

Hearings are very time consuming, so they are not compatible with the level of productivity required.

Nevertheless, hearings should be organized for some complex cases. In those circumstances, judges should have a very strict control of the hearings, fixing a precise time limit to the parties, and limiting the specific points that will be the subject of the hearing.

In fact, it is paradoxical that this important guarantee is avoided with the argument that its practice could cause an unacceptable delay in the resolution of the cases.

PART VII: COOPERATION WITH NATIONAL COURTS, POST DIRECTIVE ON ANTITRUST DAMAGES THE FUTURE OF JUDICIAL REVIEW ON BOTH NATIONAL AND EU LEVEL COOPERATION BETWEEN NATIONAL COMPETITION AUTHORITIES AND NATIONAL COURTS AND SCOPE OF JUDICIAL REVIEW ON EVIDENCE-RELATED ISSUES

■

GABRIELLA MUSCOLO[*]

SUMMARY: 1. Evidence related issues in the enforcement of antitrust rules. 2. Cooperation between public and private enforcers on the evidential grounds: from Article 15 of Regulation 1/2003 to the enforcement directive. 3. The scope of judicial review on evaluation of evidence.

I. Evidence related issues in the enforcement of antitrust rules

Competition law cases are fact intensive by nature, and the competition law judge is also a finder of the facts. Furthermore, most of relevant facts have a technical and economic nature.[1]

The White Paper[2] has already identified the parties' information asymmetry in having access to proof of relevant facts as one of the key obstacles to

---

[*] Member, Italian Competition Authority.
[1] On the issue, see A. HOWARD, *The draft directive on competition law damages: what does it mean for infringers and victims?*, in http://www.monckton.com/docs/library/AH%20Article%20Final.pdf. Council Regulation (EC) No. 1/2003 of 16 December 2002 on the implementation of the rules of competition and, if you want see G. MUSCOLO, *"Towards more effective antitrust damages actions in Europe: the Commission proposal for a Directive"*, in http://iar.agcm.it/issue/view/597.
[2] White Paper on damages actions for breach of EU antitrust rules COM (2008) 165 final: see also Commission Staff Working Paper annexed to the White Paper SEC (2008) 404 and the Impact Assessment report *"Making antitrust damages actions more effective in EU welfare impact and potential scenarios"*. A second Impact assessment has preceded the proposal for a directive. The latter indicates a directive as the most cost-efficient way of achieving the objectives of strengthening the private enforcement of antitrust rules and optimizing the interaction with public enforcement.

damages actions in competition cases. The asymmetry originates from the fact that much of the evidence the parties should bring before the Court is held by the counterparty or another person.

On 11 June 2013 the European Commission launched a proposal for a directive on actions for antitrust damages. The directive was approved with amendments by the European Parliament on 17 April 2014, signed into law on 26 November 2014 and published in the Official Journal of the European Union on 5 December 2014.

Member States need to implement the directive in their legal systems by 27 December 2016. The directive also deals with the matter of proofs.[3]

As a general rule, the option of reversing the burden of the proof (allocated in Article 2 of Regulation 1/2003) has not been exercised.

However an exception has been provided in respect of the damages quantification: Chapter V and Article 17, entitled Quantification of harm, deal with the last two issues: paragraph 2 establishes a rebuttable presumption of the existence of harm in case of a cartel infringement, mitigating the burden of proof for the claimant, especially if the provision is read together with Article 14.2 on passing on.

The rationale of the provision lies in the proximity of the evidence to the infringer more than to the victim. The former, as a result could more comfortably bear the burden of the proof and thereby avoid the most costly mechanisms of disclosure.

Article 17 does not extend the scope of the presumption to the amount of the damages and more importantly does not result in this amount being the overcharge that has been passed on in the cartel case. Nor is such effect determined by Article 12.5, that gives the court *"the power to estimate, in accordance with national procedures, the share of any overcharge that was passed on"*.[4]

Paragraph 1 contains a generic provision on the burden and the standard of proof that are required not to render *"the exercise of the right to damages practically impossible or excessively difficult"*.

---

[3] Directive 2014/104/EU of the European Parliament and of the Council on certain rules governing actions for damages under national law for infringements of the competition law provisions of the Member States and of the European Union. A draft *"Proposal for Council Directive on rules governing actions for damages for infringements of Articles 81 and 82 of the Treaty"* was circulated in the antitrust community a few years ago but has never been adopted.

[4] In Italy and in the vast litigation following AGCM decision of 28 July 2000, case 1377, *RC Auto*, the damages caused to consumers have been calculated on the amount of the overcharge paid by the plaintiffs, that the AGCM had considered to be equivalent to 20% of the premium.

On the one hand the provision seems to be aimed at lowering the standard of proof required for assessing damages, which implies a risk of under compensation or over compensation and, as a consequence, reduces the effectiveness of damages actions.

On the other hand the Commission has published the already above-mentioned Guidance Paper on the quantification of harm in antitrust damages actions, a non-binding, and not interfering with national rules and practices, instrument assisting Courts in assessing damages and possibly helping parties in settling disputes.

With respect to the issue of access to proof, the choice of the directive has fallen on a mechanism of disclosure of evidence, inspired by the EC directive 2004/48 (so called *"enforcement directive"*) in the field of Intellectual Property Law:[5] a mild form of discovery has been adopted, less broad and less costly than the US model.[6]

In this framework, a request for discovery by the interested part is subject to the following conditions: 1. the existence of *"reasonably available facts and evidence sufficient to support the plausibility"* (Article 5.1) of the claim or defense (that means elements of proof, *semiplena probatio*); 2. the relevance of the requested evidence in terms of substantiating the claim or defense; 3. the proof that the requested evidence is in the control of the other party or of a third party; 4. the specification of the requested pieces of evidence on the basis of reasonably available facts.

The last requirement is spelled out in Article 6.4 a) with regards to a request for discovery of information contained in the file of a competition authority, in which the party has the duty to detail *"the nature, subject matter or contents"* of the requested documents.

The rationale for the listed conditions is to comply with the general rule on the burden of proof on the one hand and to avoid fishing expeditions in collecting evidence on the other hand.

The European discovery is also based on the proportionality principle: the enforcement directive already provides for a proportionality limit to each measure to protect intellectual property rights, including discovery. Article 5.3 defines proportionality as the balance among *"the legitimate interests of all parties and third parties concerned"* and offers criteria for striking the balance.

---

[5] Directive 2004/48/EC of the European Parliament and of the Council of 29 April 2004 on the enforcement of intellectual property rights, *OJ* L 157, 30, o4, 2004, p. 45.
[6] The majority of EU Member States systems do not provide for a disclosure process. UK and Ireland have a broader mechanism of discovery.

These criteria are: 1. the likelihood of the alleged infringement (Article 5.3a); 2. the scope and cost of disclosure, especially for third parties (Article 5.3b); 3. confidentiality of information concerned, especially for third parties and the availability of arrangements for confidentiality protection (Article 5.3c).

What is peculiar in the European approach to discovery is that it is subject to scrutiny by the national judge, who is in charge of verifying whether request complies with the aforementioned conditions and the proportionality limit.

The paragraph 7 of Article 5, introduces the principle of the right to a fair hearing in the sub-proceeding where the discovery measure is adopted, granting the addressee of the order the right to be heard.

Article 8 provides for the power of national courts to impose sanctions on the parties to the proceedings, third parties and their legal representatives in the event of: 1. failure or refusal to comply with the disclosure order or with the order to protect confidential information; 2. destruction of relevant evidence; 3. breach of the limits on the use of evidence provided for in the Chapter.

Insofar as the refusal and the abuse of a party in the proceeding are concerned, sanctions can be significant on the evidential grounds, establishing a presumption against the non-compliant party, or for assessment of the payment of the costs of the case.

Sanctions have to be inspired to three principles: effectiveness, proportionality and deterrence.

II. Cooperation between public and private enforcers on the evidential grounds: from Article 15 of Regulation 1/2003 to Articles 5ff of the enforcement directive

Article 15.3 of Regulation 1/2003 provides for the power of NCAs to *"submit written observations"* on their own initiative – including oral observations with the Court's permission – in competition law procedures *"in the name of general interest"*. The Commission Notice on cooperation between the Court and the Commission in its wording expressly mentions *"amicus curiae"*.

It should be noted that the Impact Assessment accompanying the White Paper recommends the assistance of NCAs in collective actions not only to quantify the individual consumer's damages but also to award damages to the consumers' class as a whole.

Under Italian Law there is no special provision which expressly enable ICA to file amicus curiae briefs and, in practice, the ICA never avails itself of this option, although private enforcement actions are increasing before Italian Courts.

In Italy, recourse to this cooperation tool has been missing: scholars have tries to explained this as a consequence of strict separation between Administrative and Judicial functions. However, in my opinion it might be explained better by the absence of any compulsory notification system on pending cases which could enable the ICA to intervene in pending procedures.

The enforcement directive provides for three different mechanisms of cooperation between National Competition Authorities and National Courts on evidential grounds.

The first one is the request for disclosure of information to a NCA: Articles 6 and 7 contain detailed provisions on limits to access to the file of a NCA. Pursuant to paragraph 10 of Article 6 discovery granted by the NCA is secondary to discovery orders addressed to the parties of the proceedings or a third party

Paragraph 9 introduces a general rule of the system of disclosure of evidence contained in the file of the NCA: the rules allows disclosure, envisaging a so called white list whose contents are defined by excluding all information otherwise included in the grey and a black lists.

Paragraph 5 indeed includes a grey list, *i.e.* the list of information whose disclosure is permitted only after the end of the proceedings started by the NCA, notably: a) information prepared by third parties specifically for the proceeding; b) information that the competition authority has drawn up and sent to the parties in the course of its proceedings; and c) information related to proposed settlement submissions that have been withdrawn.

Paragraph 6 provides for a black list, composed of information (or pieces of information) whose disclosure is forbidden: a) information related to leniency programs; and b) information related to settlement submissions.

Paragraph 4 details the proportionality test related to the disclosure of evidence in the files of NCA: a) in particular the criterion of specificity of the request is set forth in relation to the nature, the matter and the contents of the documents; b) it is further required that the evidence be addressed to a proceeding before a National Court; c) it is reaffirmed that the safeguard of public enforcement is necessary.

Article 7, which provides for limits to the use of evidence obtained from the NCA by the interested parties and in the proceedings for which the evidence is obtained, has the goal of preventing abuses of right of access to evidence.

On this issue the directive gets past the European Court of Justice's ruling in the *Pfleiderer* and *Donau Chemie* cases: the parties and the Court are deprived of any right and power in relation to the admission of the disclosure of information regarding a leniency program.[7]

The rationale of these provisions is to prevent that the disclosure of evidence in the private enforcement jeopardizes the public enforcement, undermining the effects of leniency programs and hindering the on-going proceedings before NCA.[8]

The second mechanism for cooperation between public and private enforcers in facilitating parties access to proof may be identified in Article 9 of the enforcement directive: such Article dictates binding effects upon national courts of "*an infringement of competition law found by a final decision of a national competition authority or by a review court*", under the wording "*irrefutably established for the purposes of an action for damages brought before their national courts*".

The origin of such a provision lies in both English and German systems,[9] but most of continental law systems do not acknowledge binding effects for

---

[7]   See ECJ (Grand Chamber), 14 June 2011, C-360/09, *PfleidererAg v Bundeskartellamt* ruled that "*the provisions of European Union law on cartels, and in particular Council Regulation (EC) No. 1/2003 of 16 December 2002 on the implementation of the rules on competition laid down in Articles 101 TFEU and 102 TFEU, must be interpreted as not precluding a person who has been adversely affected by an infringement of European Union competition law and is seeking to obtain damages from being granted access to documents relating to a leniency procedure involving the perpetrator of that infringement. It is, however, for the courts and tribunals of the Member States, on the basis of their national law, to determine the conditions under which such access must be permitted or refused by weighing the interests protected by European Union law*". See also ECJ (First Chamber), 6 June 2013, C-536/011, *Bundeswettbewerbsbehorde v Donau Chemie Ag*, that ruled: "*European Union law, in particular the principle of effectiveness, precludes a provision of national law under which access to documents forming part of the file relating to national proceedings concerning the application of Article 101 TFEU, including access to documents made available under a leniency programme, by third parties who are not party to those proceedings with a view to bringing an action for damages against participants in an agreement or concerted practice is made subject solely to the consent of all the parties to those proceedings, without leaving any possibility for the national courts of weighing up the interests involved*".

[8]   On 23 May 2012 also the Heads of the European Competition Authorities in the resolution "*Protection of leniency material in the context of civil damages actions*" have stressed the importance of the protection of leniency material in the context of private litigation. The resolution is available at http://ec.europa.eu/competition/ecn/leniency_materialprotection en.pdf.

[9]   See in UK sections 26 and 20 in UK Enterprise Act 2002, now inserted as sections 47A e 58 in UK Competition Act and in Germany section 33 of the Competition Law.

judges of NCA decisions even if they can be challenged before a National Court.[10]

Article 9 has been shaped on the model of Article 16 in Regulation 1/2003,[11] pursuant to which the prohibition of National Courts to run counter to the decision made by the European Commission. The latter provision has been deeply debated in the antitrust community and mainly given a restrictive interpretation, as containing a *"duty not to boycott"* the Commission's decisions.[12]

The rationale of the provision is that the prohibition for the infringing undertaking to re-litigate the same issue in the follow on damages action increases efficiency in the overall enforcement of antitrust rules.

The Commission also explains that judicial review of NCA's decisions should eliminate the risk of reducing judicial protection for the undertaking

---

[10] The Association of European Competition Law Judges, in its *"Comments on the Commission's White Paper on damages actions for breach of the EC antitrust rules"*, has highlighted that *"while this proposal is supported by some of our members, reservations have been expressed by judges in some Member States that an absolute rule runs counter to national rules of evidence which permit or require the national judge freely to evaluate every piece of evidence. We consider that the national procedural rules and rules of evidence should be respected. We therefore advocate a more flexible approach. For example, rather than final decisions being treated as 'irrebuttable proof' of an infringement, there could be a rule that such decisions should be 'duly taken into account', subject to national rules of evidence, or that they be treated as 'proof' but subject to the possibility of contrary evidence being adduced"*. Especially on the Italian position see the contributions to the consultations on the White Paper of: *Presidenza del Consiglio dei Ministri, Dipartimento delle Politiche Comunitarie, Osservazioni delle Autorità Italiane concernenti il Libro Bianco della Commissione Europea in materia di risarcimento del danno per violazione delle norme antitrust comunitarie, on 16 luglio 2008; Corte Suprema di Cassazione, Osservazioni a seguito del meeting del 6 novembre 2007 con i giudici nazionali relativo al private enforcement in materia di concorrenza; Consiglio Superiore della Magistratura,* on 10 settembre 2008. See also Assonime-Associazione fra le Società Italiane per Azioni, *Comments on the White Paper on damages actions for breach of EC antitrust rules,* on 15 July 2008. All the quoted opinions agree with the Commission initiative in general but disagree with the proposal of binding effects of decisions by the NCAs.

[11] More in general, on the cooperation between the Commission and the national courts see the Commission Notice on the cooperation between the Commission and the Courts of the UE Member States in the application of Articles 81 and 82 EC, *OJ* C 101, 27 April 2004; Commission Notice on the rules of access to the Commission files in case pursuant to Articles 81 and 82 of the EC Treaty. The Explanatory Memorandum of the proposal of directive, par. 4.3, underlines that to achieve coherence between rules on access to a file of the NCA and rules on disclosure of information in a file of the Commission, the latter envisages to emend Regulation 773/2004 as well as of the explanatory Notices (Commission Regulation (EC) No. 773/2004 of 7 April 2004 relating to the conduct of proceedings by the Commission pursuant to Articles 81 and 82 of the EC Treaty, *OJ* L 123, 27 April 2004).

[12] The definition is in A. KOMNINOS, *Resolving Jurisdictional Issues,* paper presented at the *Joint Training Programme for Judges,* Jevon Institute, University College of London, London, 5 febbraio 2010. By the same author see also *EC private antitrust enforcement. Decentralised application of EC competition law by national courts,* Oxford-Portland, 2008.

concerned and violating its right of defense as enshrined in Article 48.2 of the EU Charter of Fundamental Rights.[13]

Binding effects of a decision granted in public enforcement proceedings regard the ascertainment of the infringement, and may help the parties overcome their asymmetric information in follow on actions.

However the binding effects of the NCA decision cannot extend to the link of causation or the existence or amount of damages, issues which the public enforcer cannot deal with and which seems to constitute the main object of parties' asymmetric information.[14]

Moreover, the parties obviously cannot rely on binding effects of the NCA decision in stand-alone actions, in which information might be even more asymmetric.

NCAs' assistance to National Courts represents the third cooperation mechanism between such bodies.

Article 6 paragraph 2b, indeed requires NCA to assist Courts in ascertaining whether the nature of information referred to under paragraph 2b effectively concerns leniency programs or settlements, thereby resulting in being included in the black list.

Article 6.11 enables the NCA on its own initiative to submit observation on the proportionality test on discovery.

---

[13] See Explanatory Memorandum 4.3.1.

[14] In an Italian case the District Court of Milan, 29 April 2009, *Eni and others vs Pirelli and others*, in *Int'l lis*, 3,4, 2009, con nota critica di M. STELLA, *La prima pronuncia di un tribunale italiano in un caso di c.d. follow on antitrust litigation e sul valore delle decisioni della Commissione CE in material*, the Court has ruled that: the claim for declaration: of the inexistence in the period between 20 May 1996 and 28 November 2002, of any agreement and/or any other forbidden anticompetitive practices between the producers of BR and ESBR addressed by the Commission decision 29 November 2006 in Case COMP/F/38.638 *Butadiene Rubber*; that Eni s.p.a. and other companies have never adopted forbidden anticompetitive behaviour within the sphere of the cartel ascertained by the Commission decision 29 November 2006 in case COMP/F/38.638 *Butadiene Rubber* (partially reformed by CFI); that the alleged cartel had had no effect on the product prices, were inadmissible by reason of art. 16.1 of the Modernization Regulation as they run counter to a Commission decision.
The action referred to above has been brought while proceedings were pending before the High Court of Justice between Cooper Tire & Rubber Company and others and Shell Chemical UK Limited and others, in which a decision has been granted on October 27, 2009 declining to grant a stay pursuant to art. 28 of the Judgment Regulation; it and has been defined as an Italian torpido.
The decision is a land mark case on application of art. 16; however, a remark can be made on the second part of point 3: if the provision is interpreted not as stating a positive duty of blindly following the legal reasoning of Commission decision but as founding a negative duty of not running counter it in parts in which a breach of competition rules is ascertained, statements on the point of overcharges, concerning the link of causation, are not binding for the Court.

Finally, pursuant to Article 17.3 NCA is to provide assistance to the Court in assessing damages.

The three provisions might be a good basis for implementing the *amicus curiae* mechanism.

III. The scope of judicial review on evaluation of evidence

In the Italian legal system, the standard of review of ICA decisions by Administrative Courts – *i.e.* Administrative Tribunal of Lazio on first instance and State Council on second instance – raises several problems, particularly with respect to the assessment of complex economic facts and evidences.

This judicial review issue acquires a greater relevance in light of the implementation of Article 9 of the enforcement directive on the binding effects of NCAs decisions for National Courts, in this respect, one should also note that the Commission – in its Explanatory Memorandum – has explained that judicial review of NCA's decisions should eliminate the risk of reducing judicial protection for the undertaking concerned and violating the latter's right of defense as enshrined in Article 48.2 of the EU Charter of Fundamental Rights. [15]

Less recent Italian case law (see Supreme Court ruling No. 601/1999, not an antitrust case) limited the scope of review to the so called "*intrinsic judicial review*", evaluating the technical assessment of the Authority through the technical standard it used in its technical discretion.

A recent decision (Supreme Court 2014, in an antitrust case) has restricted the power of Administrative Courts to a weak review on the mere field of the reliability of the choice made by the Authority among a wide range of possible solutions to the technical problem, avoiding a stronger review that may result in the choice of a different technical option and in a substitutive power of the Court. Interestingly, the Supreme Court's decision does not mention the ECHR case law on Article 6 of the HR Convention, especially in the Menarini case.

This decision seems to resume the old theory of para-judicial nature of the sanctioning function of the NCA and of the proceeding before it and affirms that the principle of fair trial and due process of law is implemented on the grounds of the existence of a judicial review by the Administrative Courts.

---

[15] See Explanatory Memorandum 4.3.1.

More recent case law of the Administrative Courts is consistent, as it affirms their power of intrinsic review on the merit of the case and on the use of technical discretion by the ICA, but within the framework of a *"non-substitutive"* review: in other words, the Court may opt for a different assessment of technical facts but, if so, it is only allowed to grant an annulment decision without substituting its evaluation to the ICA's one.

The standard of judicial review in the Menarini case has been recognized as suitable to guarantee a due process of law to the parties and, therefore, no clashes exist with the principle of separation of powers provided for by the Italian Constitution.

IV

CONCLUDING REMARKS

TEN YEARS OF REGULATION 1/2003:
EFFECTIVENESS, DIVERSITY, CONVERGENCE AND BEYOND

DAMIEN GERARD[*]

The 10th GCLC Annual Conference on "Ten Years of Regulation 1/2003: challenges and reform" was assuredly a rich and intense edition. More than 25 speakers have discussed a host of challenges raised by the implementation of Regulation 1/2003 over the past 10 years, and way beyond indeed. There is no point in trying to summarize the contributions of the various speakers. Instead, the following paragraphs aim to provide an impressionist account of issues discussed during the Conference and highlight their complementarity.

The Conference was prompted in the first place by the publication in July 2014 of a Commission Communication on "Ten Years of Antitrust Enforcement under Regulation 1/2003: Achievements and Future Perspectives" (the "2014 Communication"), which was very clearly presented by Alisa Sinclair of DG COMP's ECN Unit. While allowing the Commission to make a better use of its own resources, the Communication considers that Regulation 1/2003 considerably enhanced the enforcement of the EU competition rules by NCAs and national courts. As Deputy Director-General Esteva-Mosso emphasized in his contribution, the 800 cases decided over the past ten years constitute the best testimony of the effectiveness of the system put in place by Regulation 1/2003 and the best tribute possible to these officials who have designed that system in the first place. Philip Lowe reminded us of them in his opening address presenting the Modernization Regulation as the "genesis of a legal revolution", including Commissioner Van Miert and Director-General Elhermann, as well as of the context prevailing at the end of the 1990s when the White Paper on Modernization was published,

---

[*] Director, Global Competition Law Center, College of Europe. The author would like to take this opportunity to personally thank Professor Nicolas Petit for the energy he displayed during his tenure as Director of the GCLC, thereby contributing decisively to establishing the reputation of the GCLC as a unique platform promoting cutting-edge research and policy discussions in the field of competition law and economics.

marked by great challenges in terms of EU governance following the completion of the Single Market and in anticipation of the upcoming enlargement.

An important feature of the 2014 Communication, then, is the acknowledgment of the constraints arising from the remaining diversity between the enforcement frameworks in place at national level, which was largely missing from the 2009 report on the five years of functioning of Regulation 1/2003. That diversity has become increasingly apparent with the empowerment of NCAs. As the Communication put it, "[a]*fter ten years of working together, a substantial level of convergence in the application of the rules has been achieved but divergences subsist*" (§ 24). "*To enhance EU competition enforcement for the future*", it continues, "*the institutional position of NCAs needs to be reinforced while at the same time ensuring further convergence of national procedures and sanctions applying to infringements of EU antitrust rules*".

From an institutional point of view, the 2014 Communication advocates putting in place minimum guarantees of independence for NCAs, including clear and transparent appointment procedures for NCA's management, rules on conflicts of interest and incompatibilities, as well as rules ensuring that they be endowed with sufficient resources. However, on that question of independence, contributors to the Conference have essentially questioned the possibility and appropriateness of setting common rules. Adam Jasser from the Polish Competition Authority initially doubted that a "*one-size-fits-all*" definition of independence could be found. Alexis Walckiers from the Belgian Competition Authority highlighted that the arbitrage between independence and accountability was necessarily dependent on the domestic political culture. Ewoud Sakkers from the European Commission indicated that there was no such thing as a general principle of independence in EU law and pointed to the fact that sectoral regulatory frameworks rely on different set of criteria to that effect. Stephen Calkins from the Irish NCA further emphasized that there was no single model to achieve reasonable due process and that there was no *per se* antagonism between independence and the amalgamation of competences, in particular with consumer protection. And when subtly confronted with the question of the independence of the Commission, Wouter Wils recognized that it also deserved some consideration, including in view of the growing influence exercised by the European Parliament in recent years.

When it comes to procedural diversity, the 2014 Communication observes that some NCAs "*still lack fundamental powers, such as to inspect non-business premises*", that "*not all NCAs have express powers to set their enforcement priorities*" and that "*there are also differences in the scope of investigative powers*". On these issues, the 2014 Communication then considers that convergence is insufficient and that all NCAs need to have a complete set of investigative powers, the right to set enforcement priorities, and necessary enforcement and fining powers to compel compliance with investigative and decision-making powers. In this respect, Philip Mardsen from the UK Competition and Market Authority originally questioned whether such a procedural alignment was possible and at all appropriate beyond the process of soft convergence that is still unfolding. Malgorzata Modzlewska de Raad was more optimistic as she observed that, after all, the EU recently achieved (some form of) harmonization in the field of private enforcement and wondered whether the field of public enforcement was so radically different. However, from her point of view, procedural approximation also needs to address due process gaps created by the remaining diversity between domestic rules, a concern that is surprisingly absent from the 2014 Communication whereas it may in turn improve the effectiveness of enforcement and the quality and timing of decisions. That point was also raised by Denis Waelbroeck who reminded the audience of the tensions inherent to a cooperative enforcement system relying on a diversity of local enforcement frameworks. Hence, he warned against the danger of a "race to the bottom" in terms of procedural rights, contrary to the requirements of the EU Charter of Fundamental Rights and the commitment of the Union to abide by the rule of law.

Illustrating the competition authorities' concern with effectiveness, Eduardo Prieto Kessler of the Spanish Competition Authority explained how NCAs have developed over time increasingly sophisticated detection techniques to ensure the effectiveness of enforcement beyond other more classic means. Laurence Idot of the French Competition Authority then openly voiced her disagreement with the alleged divergence between NCAs' priority setting powers and the impact thereof on enforcement effectiveness, to conclude that approximating priority setting rules should not be a priority. Later on, Mario Siragusa denounced what he referred to as the "dogma" of effectiveness and its possible excesses as illustrated by the rise in commitment decisions and, conversely, by the Commission's unwillingness to invest resources in the adoption of so-called "positive decisions". Eventually, Bernd Meyring concluded the session by suggesting that the lack of recourse to interim measure decisions by the Commission could be explained by the efficient complementarity of procedures before national courts and NCAs, before which interim measures proceedings are much more common.

The third concern expressed by the 2014 Communication on Ten Years of Antitrust Enforcement under Regulation 1/2003 relates to *"ensuring that NCAs can impose effective and sufficiently deterrent fines on undertakings"* in line with the EU practice, including when it comes to parental liability and succession. In the panel devoted to fines, however, Erik Pijnacker Hordijk denounced the risk of the *ne bis in idem* issues resulting from combination of higher fines and of the territorial approach adopted by NCAs to define the scope of fines, at the suggestion of the Court of Justice. At the end, he said, business might be subject to a risk of multiple high fines only mitigated by loose requirements of "natural justice". Eric Morgan de Rivery then questioned the expansion of the concept of undertakings over the past ten years, notably to justify hardly rebuttable presumptions of parental liability, and invited the Commission to better frame that concept in a possible Regulation 1*bis*. Valérie Beaumeunier of the French Competition Authority subsequently engaged in a comparison of the French and EU settlement regimes inasmuch as they aim to achieve a balance between effectiveness and deterrence and still need to be perfected.

Naturally, both the speakers and the audience engaged in discussions going beyond the scope of the 2014 Communication. A recurring theme was the improvement of rules governing the ECN's handling of enforcement matters, including the possibility to better formalize case allocation rules in order to increase legal certainty and, as Jacques Steenbergen from the Belgian NCA suggested, the introduction of mandatory rules on information exchange in national cases.

Moving beyond the concerns and remedies discussed in the 2014 Communication, the second day of the Conference focused on observable developments in the powers of competition authorities and on the future of courts in deciding over antitrust cases. A major by-product of Modernization has indeed been the increasing sophistication of competition authorities and their development beyond a purely enforcement function. The advocacy function, in particular, as a vector of diffusion of the *"culture of competition"* promoted by the ECN, has developed into a complementary form of intervention allowing NCAs, in certain cases, to influence directly the policy-making process. For example, as Salvatore Rebecchini explained, the Italian NCA now benefits from the power to issue recommendations on existing legislation, opinions on draft legislation and specific administrative acts, as well as to challenge these acts in case of non-compliance.

Another remarkable evolution accompanying the process of modernization has been the multiplication of guidance resources published by competition authorities, thereby turning them into quasi-legislative bodies. Nicolas Petit of the University of Liège provided an overview of the *"guidance mix"* developed by the European Commission, in particular, distinguishing between generic, case-specific and hybrid guidance and discussing the Commission's reluctance to deliver positive guidance though letters or inapplicability decisions. With the increase in the powers conferred upon competition authorities comes of course a greater responsibility to deliver results and to justify the resources invested in terms of market outcomes and consumer benefits, *i.e.*, a greater need for accountability. The role of impact assessment in that respect was discussed by Ioannis Lianos of University College London as part of an evaluation narrative that is still lacking a sound theoretical framework and whose operationality may therefore still be questioned.

Historically, though, the legitimacy of competition authorities' enforcement function has primarily hinged on the judicial review of their decisions by courts of law. With the expansion of competition authorities' powers, the standards and levels of review applied by courts have been increasingly scrutinized, as well as their resources and overall ability to ensure compliance with the rule of law. The European Court of Justice's ability to do so has been particularly questioned in recent years, a subject that has been addressed heads-on by former General Court judge Santiago Soldevila Fragoso whose views were subsequently challenged by Hannes Kraemer. In particular, increasing the efficiency of the General Court – where EU Commission decisions are reviewed in first instance – by means of an increase in the number of judges was at the heart of the disagreement between the two speakers, thereby reflecting tensions internal to the European Court of Justice that have become public in recent months.

Yet, courts in the EU are also increasingly viewed as possible enforcement agents, not only review courts. To assist courts in that process, Nicholas Khan of the Commission Legal Service explained, their ability to interact with competition authorities has been significantly strengthened by Regulation 1/2003, whereas the adjudicating process in damages cases has now been partly harmonized by Directive 2014/104. As Gabriella Muscolo of the Italian Competition Authority subsequently underlined, the focus of both Regulation 1/2003 and Directive 2014/104 has rightly been on facilitating the gathering and production of evidence in cases essentially relying on technical assessments of complex facts of an economic nature. Whereas Article 15 of Regulation 1/2003 has been used increasingly by national courts in recent years, time will tell how jurisdictions will make use of the new tools provided for by Directive 2014/104 and, as a result, whether these tools will increase the effectiveness of competition law enforcement in Europe and affect the balance between the public and private components thereof.

*
* *

At the end, the Conference conveyed a seemingly shared appreciation of the achievements of Regulation 1/2003 but also a more refined understanding of the challenges it still raises and interrogations as to the reforms envisaged to tackle these challenges. In the good tradition of GCLC conferences, this tenth edition certainly contributed to the learning phase in which the Commission is currently engaged in order to assess more accurately the remaining gaps in the enforcement system put in place by Regulation 1/2003 and the appropriate means to close these gaps in the years to come. Eventually, that learning process will be informative for other policy areas where the Union has and still is experimenting with comparable forms of cooperative legal enforcement model as a way to balance unity and diversity.